SURVIVAL HINDI

How to Communicate Without
Fuss or Fear—Instantly!

Sunita Narain
Madhumita Mehrotra

TUTTLE Publishing

Tokyo | Rutland, Vermont | Singapore

The Tuttle Story: "Books to Span the East and West"

Most people are surprised to learn that the world's largest publisher of books on Asia had its humble beginnings in the tiny American state of Vermont. The company's founder, Charles E. Tuttle, belonged to a New England family steeped in publishing. And his first love was naturally books—especially old and rare editions.

Immediately after WW II, serving in Tokyo under General Douglas MacArthur, Tuttle was tasked with reviving the Japanese publishing industry. He later founded the Charles E. Tuttle Publishing Company, which thrives today as one of the world's leading independent publishers.

Though a westerner, Tuttle was hugely instrumental in bringing a knowledge of Japan and Asia to a world hungry for information about the East. By the time of his death in 1993, Tuttle had published over 6,000 books on Asian culture, history and art—a legacy honored by the Japanese emperor with the "Order of the Sacred Treasure," the highest tribute Japan can bestow upon a non-Japanese.

With a backlist of 1,500 titles, Tuttle Publishing is more active today than at any time in its past—inspired by Charles Tuttle's core mission to publish fine books to span the East and West and provide a greater understanding of each.

Published by Tuttle Publishing, an imprint of Periplus Editions (HK) Ltd.

www.tuttlepublishing.com

Copyright © 2012 Periplus Editions (HK) Ltd

All rights reserved. No part of this publication may be reproduced or utilized in any form or by any means, electronic or mechanical, including photocopying, recording, or by any information storage and retrieval system, without prior written permission from the publisher.

Library of Congress Cataloging-in-Publication Data for this title is available.

ISBN 978-0-8048-4279-2

First edition
15 14 13 12   5 4 3 2 1   1203CP

Distributed by

North America, Latin America & Europe
Tuttle Publishing
364 Innovation Drive
North Clarendon, VT 05759-9436 U.S.A.
Tel: 1 (802) 773-8930
Fax: 1 (802) 773-6993
info@tuttlepublishing.com
www.tuttlepublishing.com

Asia Pacific
Berkeley Books Pte. Ltd.
61 Tai Seng Avenue #02-12
Singapore 534167
Tel: (65) 6280-1330
Fax: (65) 6280-6290
inquiries@periplus.com.sg
www.periplus.com

Printed in Singapore

TUTTLE PUBLISHING® is a registered trademark of Tuttle Publishing, a division of Periplus Editions (HK) Ltd.

ACKNOWLEDGMENTS

ॐ वाक्देवययी च: विदमहे
विरिन्जि पत्निययी च: धीमहे
तन्नो वाणी प्रचोदयात्

Om, Let me meditate on the goddess of speech,
Oh, wife of Lord Brahma, give me higher intellect,
and let Goddess of "Vani" illuminate my mind.

With the blessings of Goddess Saraswati, our fathers, the late Dr. Lalit Behari Lall Mathur and Mr. K.K. Sarkar, and our mothers, Mrs. Sarla Mathur and Mrs. Bani Sarkar, this book, *Survival Hindi,* has finally taken shape and is ready to help those who would like to embark on a journey to explore the rich and diverse culture of India.

We would especially like to thank Sameer Narain and Rakhi Narain, whose insight, intellect, and indispensable typing abilities helped us to finish this book on time; as well as Rishi Narain for sharing his experience as a foreigner in India.

We also thank all of our family and friends, who lent their tremendous support, in one way or another, to compile this work.

Contents

Acknowledgments 3
Welcome 7

INTRODUCTION 8
The Alphabet 8
Pronunciation Guide 9
Notes on How Hindi Works 15

PART 1 Common Expressions & Key Words
Greetings 17
Introductions; Introducing Others 19
Titles
    Personal 21
    Academic 22
    Business and Professional 23
    Trade / Skilled Worker 28
Common Expressions and Phrases 30
Any Questions? Just Ask! 36
Asking for Toilets and Restrooms 43
Asking for Help 44

PART 2 Numbers, Time, and Other "Basics"
Cardinal Numbers 47
Ordinal Numbers 48
Days of the Week 51

Which Day? 52

Months 53

Dates 54

Seasons 54

Weather 55

Asking and Telling Time 57

Family 63

Parts of the Body 65

Map Directions 67

PART 3 Getting Around

At the Airport 68

Hiring a Taxi or Autorickshaw 70

Renting a Vehicle 73

Hiring a Cycle Rickshaw 75

At a Train Station 75

Metro Rail 80

Traveling by Bus 81

Asking for Directions & Locations 82

PART 4 Emergencies and Essentials; Lodging

At the Police Station 86

Medical Emergencies 88

Accommodations 91

Making Reservations 92

Banking and Money 93

PART 5 In a Restaurant; Out and About

Ordering Food and Paying the Bill 95

Shopping 99

Purchasing & Bargaining 101
At a Book Store 104
At a Clothing Store 106
Measurements & Sizes.. 108
At the Post Office... 109
At a Pharmacy... 112
At the Barbershop 114
At the Beauty Salon.. 116
Using the Telephone / Cell Phones.................... 117

PART 6 Enjoying India
Holidays 119
Holiday Greetings 122
Top Destinations in India.................................. 124
Sightseeing 127

PART 7 Key Names & Signs
India's States and Union Territories.................... 132
Common Signs 134
Road Signs 137

PART 8 Additional Vocabulary
Food Terms 138
General Word List... 143

WELCOME!

We welcome you with the traditional Hindi greeting "**Namaste**," which means "I bow to you," and are very pleased to take you on a short journey through Hindi, the official language of India.

With a little bit of instruction about how Hindi works, we will help you properly communicate with the locals in India. We'll help you speak to others on various basic "survival" topics, such as introducing yourself, asking for directions, ordering food, paying a bill, bargaining with a local vendor, and even reporting an incident to police. Essentially, all the things you might find most useful to say are in this survival guide for getting by in Hindi.

Our years of experience teaching Hindi to non-natives, along with vast personal interactions with foreigners in India, have armed us with an abundance of detailed cultural and linguistic information. We hope that here in *Survival Hindi*, it will serve to ease your journey, and give you a sense of joy in more fully understanding India and its people. Let's begin!

INTRODUCTION
"The Language of the Gods"

Hindi, spoken today by nearly 500 million people as a first language, is derived from the ancient language Sanskrit, considered one of the most intriguing, musical, and divine languages ever spoken. Sanskrit is recognized by its unique written alphabet, *Devanagari*, meaning "Language of the Gods." Hindi retains the use of *Devanagari* today as its own alphabet. Of the numerous daughter tongues originating from Sanskrit, Hindi is the most widespread, and is one of the 22 official languages of the Republic of India.

According to Hindu mythology, the human voice, or *vak*, was provided to mankind by the goddess Sarasvati, who presided over wisdom, knowledge, learning, music, and the arts. *Vak* is also often personified as a separate goddess commonly identified with *Bharati* (Bhaar-tee) or *Sharda* (Shaar-daa), the goddess of speech. The term *vak* is a cognate to the modern English word *voice* (Latin *vox*), and is derived from the verbal root *vac-*, meaning "to speak, tell, utter." It also shares meaning with such words as "speech" and "talk."

The Alphabet

Hindi script (Devanagari) is made up of 46 basic characters; there are 33 consonants and 12 vowels. Each character stands for one syllable.

The Devanagari script represents the phonetics of the Hindi language. This means that Hindi is spoken the same way it is spelled. Its alphabet is scientifically arranged.

Along with the written Hindi, each phrase in this book offers you an easy, English-based transliteration to help you pronounce it. Here's how it works.

Pronunciation Guide

Long Vowels

ā (*aa*) c<u>a</u>r   ī (*ee*) b<u>ee</u>t   é (*a*) g<u>a</u>te   ū (*oo*) f<u>oo</u>l

Short Vowels

i (<u>i</u>t)   u (p<u>u</u>t, f<u>oo</u>t)

Nasal Sounds

A dot over a consonant or a vowel, or an "n" in parentheses, indicates a nasal sound. Imagine you are half-saying an "n" or "m" sound after that syllable.

hai(n)   **mei(n)**

ṁ as in "ṁandir" *(<u>mun</u>-dir)*

é̇ as in "lé̇gé" *(<u>layn</u>-gay)*

Sometimes you'll see a nasal ending after a long vowel:

ā̇ as in "sārdiyā̇" *(saard-iy<u>aan</u>)*

Vowels

Hindi Independent Vowel	Trans-literation	Vowel symbols with consonants	Position as a dependent vowel	Pronounced as
अ	**a**	क्+अ = क ka	Inherent in all the consonants	b<u>u</u>t, c<u>u</u>t
आ	**ā**	क+आ = का kā	Long sound "ā" follows a conso-nant	st<u>a</u>r, b<u>a</u>r
इ	**i**	क्+इ = कि ki	Precedes a consonant	<u>i</u>t, k<u>i</u>t
ई	**ī**	क्+ई = की kī	Follows a consonant	m<u>ea</u>t, s<u>ea</u>t
उ	**u**	क्+उ = कु ku र्+उ = रु ru	Placed under/to the side of a conso-nant	p<u>u</u>t, f<u>oo</u>t r<u>u</u>pee
ऊ	**ū**	क्+ऊ = कू kū र्+ऊ = रू rū	Placed under/to the side of a conso-nant	f<u>oo</u>l, t<u>oo</u>t r<u>oo</u>t
ऋ	**ri**	क्+ऋ = कृ kri	Placed under a consonant	g<u>ri</u>p, g<u>ri</u>t

Hindi Independent Vowel	Trans-literation	Vowel symbols with consonants	Position as a dependent vowel	Pronounced as
ए	é	क+ए = के ké	Placed on top of a consonant	gate, bate
ऐ	ai	क+ऐ = कै kai	Placed on top of a consonant	sat, rat
ओ	o	क+ओ = को ko	Placed on to the right side of a consonant	goat, boat
औ	au	क+औ = कौ kau	Placed on to the right side of a consonant	caught, bought
अ	uṅ	क+अ ं = कं kung	Placed on top of a consonant as a nasal symbol	blunt, stunt

Consonants

Each consonant of the Devanagari (Hindi) script contains the inherent vowel "*a*" in it. Without its help no consonant is considered to be complete. There are 33 consonants in the Devanagari script.

We can look at them organized according to the kinds of sounds they are—and where in the mouth the sounds are made.

Position in the mouth	Voiceless un-aspirated	Voiceless aspirated	Voiced un-aspirated	Voiced aspirated	Nasal
Velar/ guttural *Back of mouth*	क ca**k**e **k**a	ख **c**ar **kh**a	ग **g**ame **g**a	घ **gh**ost **gh**a	ङ ba**ng ng**
Palatal *Mid-point in mouth*	च sat**ch**el **ch**a	छ mat**Ch** **Chh**a	ज **j**ungle **j**a	झ marr**iage** **Jhh**a	ञ **ny**a
Retroflex *Tongue curled back in mouth*	ट **T**rump **T**a	ठ eigh**T** **Thh**a	ड **D**ig **D**a	ढ ba**D** **Dhh**a	ण **rN**
Dental *Tongue between teeth*	त **t**a	थ ari**th**metic **thh**a	द mo**th**er **d**a	ध **dhh**a	न Mo**n** day **n**a

Position in the mouth	Voiceless un-aspirated	Voiceless aspirated	Voiced un-aspirated	Voiced aspirated	Nasal
Labial *From the lips*	प gap*p* *p*a	फ *p*ower *phh*a	ब *bubb*le *b*a	भ a*bh*or *bhh*a	म *m*an *m*a
Semi-vowels	य ma*y*or *y*a	र b*r*ain *r*a	ल *l*eg *l*a	व *v*an *v*a/*w*a	
Sibilants and glottal stops	श a*sh* *sh*a	ष ba*Sh* *Sh*a	स Mar*s* *s*a	ह *h*ug *h*a	
Conjuncts	क्ष mo*ksha* *ksha*	त्र man*tr*a *tr*a	ज्ञ *gy*a		
Loaned letters (Persian, Arabic)	क़ *Q*uran	ख़ ban*k*	ग़ (no similar sound in English)	फ़ *f*lower	ज़ A*z*tec

A Bit More About Pronunciation...

You'll see the pronunciation of a word or a phrase written in italics after it: **Hindi** (***hin-dee***). The words are broken into syllables, separated by a hyphen (-). Keep in mind that these hyphenated English phonetics should be pronounced in a smooth, even flow. Read them out loud several times to train your tongue and lips in making the proper sounds smoothly. Here are notes on a few special sounds:

"**Chh**"—uppercase *C* with lowercase *hh*—is used for a sound where aspiration is needed, as you hear in the English word *"cat<u>ch</u>."* The lowercase **"ch"** is used for the regular non-aspirated sound, as in *"sat<u>ch</u>el."*

You will notice that at many places we have used the uppercase letter **"T"** in a word; this means that the letter **"T"** is a retroflex sound. It is pronounced with the tip of the tongue turned back against the roof of the mouth—you can feel this by saying the word *"re<u>tr</u>oflex."* The lowercase **"t,"** on the other hand, indicates that the sound is dental; you say it with the tongue against the upper teeth, as in *"<u>t</u>ee."*

The uppercase **"D"** is used to indicate the retroflex *d* sound as in *"ma<u>d</u>, be<u>d</u>"*; whereas the lowercase **"d"** is used to indicate the sound of *th* in the English *"<u>th</u>ough"* or *"<u>th</u>e."*

In Hindi, there is no distinction between a *v* and a *w* sound. So the letters **"v"** and **"w"** may be used interchangeably to indicate that sound.

Notes on How Hindi Works

Word Order
In English you might say, "The boy is eating in the room." But the word order in Hindi grammar is Subject + Object + Verb. So in Hindi you would say, "The boy room in eating is."

Nouns
Hindi distinguishes two *genders* (male or female), two *numbers* (singular or plural), and three *cases* or forms (the direct, oblique, and vocative). So the form a noun takes, when you are saying or writing it, depends on those factors. You'll see these differences called to your attention in some sections of the book.

Genders
The genders in Hindi are highly significant. There is no neuter gender in Hindi: every noun is either masculine or feminine. The gender of a noun determines its masculine, feminine and plural forms, and also the appropriate way to modify adjectives and participles.

Adjectives
Since Hindi is a gender-oriented language, an adjective must agree with the noun it's describing. So, Hindi adjectives have masculine, feminine and plural forms. To help you choose the correct one depending on what you want to say, we've used "/" to show those options.

Masculine is indicated by (m.)
Feminine is indicated by (f.)
Plural is indicated by (pl.)

Verbs

We have provided the imperative forms of verbs for your convenience. As a command a verb will end in the **"o"** sound, and as a request it will end in "**-i-yay.**" Here are a few examples:

As a command:
 Listen. **Suno.** *(Su-no)*
 Stop. **Ruko** *(Ru-ko)*

As a request:
 Please listen. **Suniyé.** *(Su-ni-yay)*
 Please stop. **Rukiyé** *(Ru-ki-yay)*

Hindi verbs are conjugated according to the gender of the subject in the direct case, and in the indirect case it conjugates with the object of the sentence. In this book you will find that if the subject of a direct-case sentence or a phrase such as "I am going" is a female noun, then the sentence will end in long ī (*ee*) vowel with an auxiliary verb. And if it is a male subject, then it will end in long ā (*aa*).

PART ONE

Common Expressions & Key Words

GREETINGS

▶ Hello / Goodbye
Namasté नमस्ते / **Namaskār** नमस्कार (to anyone, including known or unknown elders)
(Num-us-tay / Num-us-kaar)

Pranām प्रणाम (to elderly people)
(Pr-un-aam)

▶ Good morning
Shubh prabhāt शुभ प्रभात
(Shu-bh pr-bhaat)

▶ Good night
Shubh rātrī शुभ रात्रि
(Shu-bh-raat-ree)

▶ Nice to meet you.
Āpsé milkar khushī huī. (formal)
आपसे मिलकर खुशी हुई।
(Aap-say mil-kerr-khu-shee hu-ee.)

Tum sé milkar khushī huī. (informal)
तुमसे मिलकर खुशी हुई।
(Tum-say mil-kerr khu-shee hu-ee.)

▶ Nice to meet you too.
  Mujhé bhī. मुझे भी|
  (Mu-jh-a bhee.)

▶ See you later.
  Phir milégé. फिर मिलेंगे|
  (Phir mil-a-ng-ay.)

▶ See you tomorrow.
  Kal milégé. कल मिलेंगे|
  (K-ul mil-a-ng-ay.)

▶ How are you?
  Āp kaisé hai(n)? आप कैसे हैं? (formal, to m.)
  (Aap kay-say hain?)

  Āp kaisī hai(n)? आप कैसी हैं? (formal, to f.)
  (Aap kay-see hain?)

  Tum kaisé ho? तुम कैसे हो? (informal, to m.)
  (Tu-m ka-say ho)

  Tum kaisī ho? तुम कैसी हो? (informal, to f.)
  (Tu-m kay-see ho?)

Remember, for many phrases you'll see options, because
in Hindi how you say something may be different depending on whether you're male or female. If you are male, you
should choose the option labeled "male speaker" (or "m.
spkr"); and if you are female, choose the option for "female
speaker" ("f. spkr").

▶ I'm fine.
Mai(n) Thīk hū̃. मैं ठीक हूँ।
(Main Thh-eek hoon.)

▶ And you?
Āp sunāiyé. / Āp batāiyé. आप सुनाइये / आप बताइये।
(Aap su-n-aa-e-yay / Aap ba-taa-e-yay.)

▶ Thank you.
Dhanyavād. धन्यवाद। (Hindi)
(dh-nya-waad.)

Shukhriyā. शुक्रिया। (Urdu)
(Shuk-re-yaa.)

Although India's main language is Hindi, there is a substantial amount of Urdu (a language widely spoken in Pakistan) vocabulary that is used in India on a day-to-day basis. Therefore, it would be politically correct to use **Shukhriya** as another way to say "Thank you."

INTRODUCTIONS

▶ What is your name?
Āpkā nām kyā hai? आपका नाम क्या है? (formal)
(Aap-kaa naam kyaa hai?)

Tumhārā nām kyā hai? (informal)
तुम्हारा नाम क्या है?
(Tu-m-haa-raa naam kyaa hai?)

- ▶ My name is ___.
  Mérā nām ___ hai. मेरा नाम__है|
  (May-raa-naam ___ hai.)

- ▶ Where are you from?
  Āp kahā̃ sé hai(n)? आप कहाँ से हैं?
  (Aap kah-haan say hain?)

- ▶ I am from *(insert place)*.
  Mai(n) ___ sé hū̃. मैं__से हूँ|
  (Main ___ say hoon.)

INTRODUCING OTHER PEOPLE

- ▶ This is my wife.
  Yéh mérī patnī hai(n). ये मेरी पत्नि हैं|
  (Yeh may-ree pat-nee hain.)

- ▶ This is my husband.
  Yéh méré pati hai(n). ये मेरे पति हैं|
  (Yeh may-ray pa-ti hain.)

- ▶ These are my/our children.
  Yeh méré/hamāré bachché hai(n). ये हमारे बच्चे हैं|
  (Yeh may-ray/hum-aa-ray bah-ch-chay hain.)

- ▶ This is my friend.
  Yéh mérā/mérī dost hai. ये मेरा / मेरी दोस्त है|
  (Yeh may-raa/may-ree tho-st hai.)

▶ This is my father.
   Yéh méré pitā-jī hai(n). / pāpa hai(n).
   ये मेरे पिताजी हैं / ये मेरे पापा हैं।
   (Yeh may-ray pitaa-jee hain / paa-paa hain.)

▶ This is my mother.
   Yéh mérī mātā-jī hai(n). / mā̃ hai(n).
   ये मेरी माताजी हैं / माँ हैं।
   (Yeh may-ree maa-taa-jee/ maa-n hai(n).)

Remember, for many phrases you'll see options, because in Hindi how you say something may be different depending on whether the speaker is male or female. This difference, and other word options that are possible, are sometimes marked in this book with a slash: "/".

PERSONAL TITLES

▶ Mr.
   Shrī, Shrīmān श्री, श्रीमान
   (shr-ee, shr-ee-maan)

▶ Sir
   Sir, Sāhab, Sāhib सर, साहब, साहिब
   (sir, saa-hub, saa-hib)

▶ Mrs.
   Shrīmati श्रीमति
   (shr-ee-mutti)

▶ Miss / Ms.
   Sushrī, Kumārī सुश्री, कुमारी
   (su-shr-ee, ku-maa-ree)

ACADEMIC TITLES

▶ President
Adhyaksh अध्यक्ष
(adh-yuk-sh)

▶ Chancellor
Kulpati कुलपति
(kul-pa-ti)

▶ Principal (of a school; male)
Pradhānāchārya प्रधानाचार्य
(pr-dhaa-naa-chaar-ee-ya)

▶ Principal (of a school; female)
Pradhānāchāriyā प्रधानाचार्या
(pr-dhaa-naa-chaar-ee-yaa)

▶ Principal (of a college; male)
Prāchārya प्राचार्य
(praa-chaar-ya)

▶ Principal (of a college; female)
Prāchariyā प्राचार्या
(praa-chaar-yaa)

▶ Department Head
Vibhāgādhyaksh विभागाध्यक्ष
(vi-bhaa-gaa-dhy-ksh)

▶ Professor
Prādhyāpak प्राध्यापक
(praa-dhyaa-puk)

- ► Lecturer
  Vyākhyātā व्याख्याता
  (vyaa-khyaa-taa)

- ► Teacher (male)
  Shikshak, Adhyāpak, Guru शिक्षक, अध्यापक, गुरू
  (shick-shuk, adh-yaa-puk)

- ► Teacher (female)
  Shikshikā, Adhyāpikā शिक्षिका, अध्यापिका
  (shick-shick-aa, adh-yaa-pik-aa)

- ► Student (male)
  Vidyārthī, Chātra विद्यार्थी, छात्र
  (vidh-yaar-thee, Chhaa-trah)

- ► Student (female)
  Vidyārthī, Chātrā विद्यार्थी, छात्रा
  (vidh-yaar-thee, Chhaa-traa)

BUSINESS AND PROFESSIONAL TITLES

- ► accountant
  lékhākār लेखाकार
  (lay-khaa-kaar)

- ► artist
  kalākār कलाकार
  (kul-aa-kaar)

▶ attorney
vakīl, adhivaktā वकील, अधिवक्ता
(vuk-eel, udh-i-vuck-taa)

▶ businessman
vyāpārī व्यापारी
(vyaa-paa-ree)

▶ clerk
bābū बाबू
(baa-boo)

▶ consultant
salāhkār सलाहकार
(sul-haa-kaar)

▶ doctor
chikitsak चिकित्सक
(chi-kit-sak)

▶ driver
chālak चालक
(chaa-lak)

▶ editor
sampādak सम्पादक
(sum-paa-dak)

▶ engineer
abhiyantā, ingineer अभियंता, इंजीनियर
(abhi-yun-taa, in-jee-near)

▶ factory owner
mil mālik मिल मालिक
(mill-maa-lik)

▶ general manager
mahāprabandhak महाप्रबंधक
(ma-haa-pra-bundh-uk)

▶ government officer
sarkārī adhīkārī सरकारी अधिकारी
(sir-kaa-ree adhi-kaa-ree)

▶ government worker
sarkārī karmchārī सरकारी कर्मचारी
(sir-ka-ree kar-um-chaa-ree)

▶ governor
rājyapāl राज्यपाल
(raa-jy-paal)

▶ guide
gāid गाइड
(gaa-id)

▶ journalist
patrakār पत्रकार
(putt-ra-kaar)

▶ laborer
majdūr, kārīgar मजदूर, कारीगर
(muj-doo-r, kar-ee-gerr)

▶ librarian
pustakālayādhyaksh पुस्तकालयाध्यक्ष
(pusta-kaa-luyaa-dhy-ksh)

▶ mayor
mahāpaur महापौर
(mah-haa-pawr)

▶ mechanic
mistrī मिस्त्री
(mist-ree)

▶ musician
sangītkār संगीतकार
(sung-eet-kar)

▶ nurse
nurse नर्स
(ner-s)

▶ President (country's)
rāshTrapati राष्ट्रपति
(raa-sh-Tr-putti)

▶ president (of an organization)
adhyaksh अध्यक्ष
(uh-dh-yuk-sh)

▶ prime minister
pradhān mantrī प्रधानमंत्री
(pra-dhaan munt-ree)

▶ scientist
  vaigyānik वैज्ञानिक
  (vag-yaa-nik)

▶ secretary
  sachivālya सचिवालय
  (such-iv-aa-luy)

▶ sportsperson
  khilādī खिलाड़ी
  (khil-aa-rDee)

▶ technician
  taknīshian तकनीशियन
  (tuck-nee-she-un)

▶ tourist
  parytak पर्यटक
  (puryuh-tuck)

▶ translator
  anuvādak अनुवादक
  (unu-vaa-duk)

▶ vice-president
  UprāshTrapati उपराष्ट्रपति
  (oop-raash-Tr-putti)

▶ writer
  lékhak लेखक
  (lay-khak)

TRADE / SKILLED WORKER TITLES

▶ tea vendor
chāywālā चायवाला
(chaay-waa-laa)

▶ fruit seller
phalwālā फलवाला
(ph-ul-waa-laa)

▶ vegetable seller
sabzīwālā सब्ज़ीवाला
(sub-z-waa-laa)

▶ barber
nāyī नाई
(naa-yee)

▶ cobbler
mōchī मोची
(mow-chee)

▶ washerman
dhōbī धोबी
(dho-bee)

▶ tailor
darzī दर्ज़ी
(der-zee)

▶ janitor
méhtar मेहतर, **safāī karmchārī** सफ़ाई कर्मचारी
(meh-ter, suf-aa-ee karm-chaa-ree)

- maid
  naukarānī नौकरानी
  (knaw-ker-aa-nee)

- servant
  naukar नौकर
  (knaw-ker)

- nanny
  āyā आया
  (aa-yaa)

- milkman
  dūdhwālā दूधवाला
  (doo-dh-waa-laa)

- milkmaid
  dūdhwālī दूधवाली
  (doo-dh-waa-lee)

COMMON EXPRESSIONS
AND PHRASES

▶ Do you speak English?
Kyā āp angrézī bolté hai(n)? (to m. audience) /
Kyā āp angrézi boltī hai(n)? (to f. audience)
क्या आप अंग्रेज़ी बोलते हैं / बोलती हैं?
(Kyaa aap ung-ray-z bol-__tay__ hain /
Kyaa aap ung-ray z bol-__tee__ hain?)

Remember, for many phrases you'll see options, indicated
by a slash: "/".

These several phrases are good examples of that! Just
choose the correct option for your situation.

▶ I have understood.
Mai(n) samajh gayā. (m. spkr) / **Mai(n) samajh
gayī.** (f. spkr)
मैं समझ गया / मैं समझ गयी।
(Main sum-ujh guh-__yaa__ / Mai(n) sum-ujh guh-__yee__.)

▶ I did not understand.
Mai(n) samjhā nahī̇. (m. spkr) / **Mai(n) samjhī
nahī̇.** (f. spkr)
मैं समझा नहीं / मैं समझी नहीं।
*(Main sum-jh__aa__ na-heen / Main sum-jh__ee__ na-
heen.)*

► Please speak slowly.
Kripyā thorDā dhīré boliyé. कृपया थोड़ा धीरे बोलिए|
(Kri-pa-yaa tho-raa dhee-ray-bol-i-yay.)

► Please write it down.
Kripayā yeh likh dījīyé. कृपया यह लिख दीजिए|
(Kri-pa-yaa yeh likh dee-ji-yay.)

► What is this called in Hindi?
Isé Hindī mein kyā kaihté hai(n)?
इसे हिन्दी में क्या कहते हैं?
(Is-a Hindi may kyaa kah-tay hain?)

► Thank you very much.
Āpkā bahut-bahut dhanyavād.
आपका बहुत-बहुत धन्यवाद
(Aap-kaa bahut bahut dh-nya-vaad.)

Note: In India people don't usually respond to "thank you very much" by saying "you're welcome." Instead they would simply say "It's OK."

► It's OK.
Koi bāt nahī. कोई बात नहीं|
(Ko-ee baat na-heen.)

► Excuse me.
Māf kījīyé / Kshmā kījīyé. माफ़ कीजिए / क्षमा कीजिए|
(Maa-f kee-ji-yay / Sh-maa kee-ji-yay.)

► I am sorry / sorry to disturb you.
Māfī / Kshmā chāhtā hū̃. माफ़ी / क्षमा चाहता हूँ|
(m. spkr) *(Maa-fee chaa-h-taa hoon / Sh-maa chaa-h-tee hoon.)*
Māfī / Kshmā chāhtī hū̃. माफ़ी / क्षमा चाहती हूँ|
(f. spkr) *(Maa-fee chaa-h-taa hoon / Sh-maa chaa-h-tee hoon.)*

► Just a moment please.
Ék minat rukiyé. एक मिनट रुकिए|
(Ayk min-uT ru-ki-yay.)

► Hello! (to attract someone's attention)
Suniyé! सुनिए!
(Su-ni-yay!)

► I see!
Oh! ओह!
(O-h!)

► I don't want anything else. / No more, thank you.
Mujhé aur kuch nahī̃ chāhiyé. / Bas, dhanyavād.
मुझे और कुछ नहीं चाहिए / बस धन्यवाद|
(Mujh-ay or ku-Chh na-heen chaa-hi-yay / Bas dh-ny-vaad.)

► Is it all right?
Kyā yéh Thhīk hai? क्या यह ठीक है?
(Kyaa yeh Thh-eek hai?)

► I don't want / need it.
Mujhé nahī̃ chāhiyé. मुझे नहीं चाहिए|
(Mujh-ay na-heen chaa-hi-yay.)

► Really! Is that right?
Wākaī! Sahī mei(n)? वाक़ई! सही में?
(Vaa-ka-ee! Sa-hee mein?)

► Where is the toilet / restroom?
Bāthrūm kahằ hai? / Shauchālaya kahằ hai?
बाथरूम कहाँ है / शौचालय कहाँ है?
(Baa-th room ka-haan hai / Shaw-chaa-luy ka-haan hai?)

► I am here on business.
Main yahằ kām sé āyā hǔ. मैं यहाँ काम से आया हूँ
(Main ya-haan kaam say aa-yaa hoon.)

► I am tired.
Mai(n) thak gayā hǔ. मैं थक गया हूँ (m. spkr)
(Main th-uck ga-yaa hoon.)

Mai(n) thak gayī hǔ. मैं थक गयी हूँ (f. spkr)
(Main th-uck ga-yee hoon.)

► I am sick.
Mai(n) bīmār hǔ. मैं बीमार हूँ
(Main bee-maar hoon.)

Another option is:
Mérī tabīyat khrāb hai. मेरी तबियत ख़राब है
(May-ree tab-ee-yat kh-raab hai.)

► I've got a bad cold.
Mujhé bahut téz zukām ho gayā hai.
मुझे बहुत तेज़ ज़ुकाम हो गया है
(Mujh-ay ba-hut tayz zu-kaam ho ga-yaa hai.)

► I am thirsty.

Two options:

Mujhé pyās lagī hai. / Mujhé pyās lag rahī hai.
मुझे प्यास लगी है | मुझे प्यास लग रही है|
(Mujh-ay pyaa-s lag-ee hai / Mujh-ay pyaa-s lag ra-hee hai.)

► I am hungry.

Two options:

Mujhé bhūkh lagī hai. / Mujhé bhūkh lag rahi hai.
मुझे भूख लगी है | मूझे भूख लग रही है|
(Mujh-ay bhoo-kh lag-ee hai / Mujh-ay bhoo-kh lag ra-hee hai.)

► I'll see you later.
Mai(n) tumsé phir milūngā. मैं तुमसे फिर मिलूँगा| (m. spkr)
(Main tu-m-say phir mil-oon-gaa.)

Mai(n) āpsé phir milūngī. मैं आपसे फिर मिलूँगी| (f. spkr)
(Main aap-say phir mil-oon-gee.)

► Do you have time / Are you free?
Kyā āpké pās samay hai? / Kyā āpké pās fursat hai? क्या आप के पास समय | फुर्सत है?
(Kyaa aap-kay paas sum-ay hai / Kyaa aap-kay paas fursat hai?)

► Can you do me a favor?
  Kyā mérā ék kām kar sakté hai(n)? (to a m. audience; formal/polite)
  क्या मेरा एक काम कर सकते हैं?
  (Kyaa may-raa ayk kaam ker suk-tay hain?)
  Kyā mérā ék kām kar sakti hai(n)? (to a f. audience; formal/polite)
  क्या मेरा एक काम कर सकतीं हैं?
  (Kyaa may-raa ayk kaam ker suk-ti hain?)

► Don't worry.
  Chintā mat karo. (informal) / **kījiyé.** (formal/polite)
  चिन्ता मत करो / चिन्ता मत कीजिए
  (Chin-taa mat kero / Chin-taa mat kee-ji-yay.)

► Everything is OK.
  Sab Thik hai. सब ठीक है
  (Sub Thheek hai.)

► How was your trip?
  Āpkī yātrā kaisī rahī? आप की यात्रा कैसी रही?
  (Aap-kee yaat-raa kai-see ra-hee?)

► How old are you?
  Āpkī umr kyā hai? आप की उम्र क्या है?
  (Aap-kee umr kyaa hai?)

► What a coincidence!
  Kyā itéfāk hai / sàyog hai!
  क्या इत्तफ़ाक़ है / क्या संयोग है!
  (Kyaa itt-a faaq hai / Kyaa sanyog hai!)

▶ What happened?
  Kyā hua? क्या हुआ?
  (Kyaa hu-aa?)

▶ What is the matter?
  Kyā bāt hai? क्या बात है?
  (Kyaa baat hai?)

Keep in mind that the hyphenated English phonetics shown in this book should be pronounced in a smooth, even flow. Read them out loud several times to train your tongue and lips in making the proper sounds smoothly.

ANY QUESTIONS? JUST ASK!

> DO, DID, IS, WILL...? or CAN, WAS...? **Kyā** क्या

The answer to these types of questions is either:

▶ Yes **hā̃** हाँ *(haan)* or

▶ No **nahī̃** नहीं *(na-heen)*.

When you ask a question, end the sentence on a higher note, just as you do in your own language.

▶ Do you know where this place is?
  kyā āpko mālūm hai yeh jagah kahā̃ hai?
  क्या आपको मालूम है यह जगह कहाँ है?
  (Kyaa aap-ko maa-loom hai yeh jug-eh ka-haan hai?)

▶ Do you know the way to the hotel?
Kyā āpko hotel kā rāstā patā hai?
क्या आपको होटल का रास्ता पता है?
(Kyaa aap-ko hotel kaa raas-taa pa-taa hai?)

▶ Do you have a western-style toilet?
Kyā āpké yahā̃ kamod vālā bāthroom hai?
क्या आपके यहाँ कमोड वाला बाथरूम है?
(Kyaa aap-kay ya-haan come-ode vaa-laa baa-th-room hai?)

▶ Do you have a cold Bisleri water bottle?
Kyā āpké pās bislerī kī thandé panī kī botal hai?
क्या आपके पास बिसलैरी की ठंडे पानी की बोतल है?
(Kyaa aap-kay paas bis-leri kee th-un-day paa-nee kee bo-tull hai?)

"Bisleri" is a brand name for bottled mineral water in India.

▶ Do you have ___ in a larger size?
Kyā ___ āpké pās barDé size méin hai?
क्या __ आपके पास बड़े साइज़ में है?
(Kyaa ___ aa-p-kay paas ba-rD-ay size mein hai?)

▶ Is the train on time?
Kyā train time par hai?
क्या ट्रेन टाइम पर है?
(Kyaa train time per hai?)

▶ Can you tell us the way?
Kyā āp haméi(n) rāstā batā sakté hain?
क्या आप हमें रास्ता बता सकते हैं?
(Kyaa aap hum-ein raas-taa but-aa suk-tay hain?)

▶ Is this train / bus going to ___?
  Kyā yéh train/bus ___ jā rahī hai?
  क्या यह ट्रेन / बस ___ जा रही है?
  (Kyaa yeh train / bus ___ jaa-rahee hai?)

▶ Can I sit here?
  Kyā mai(n) yahă̆ baiTh jāū̆?
  क्या मैं यहाँ बैठ जाऊँ?
  (Kyaa main ya-haan bai-Thh jaa-oon?)

WHAT...? **Kyā** क्या

▶ What is this?
  Yeh kyā hai? यह क्या है / ये क्या है?
  (Yeh kyaa hai?)

▶ This is ___.
  Yeh ___ hai. यह / ये ___ है।
  (Yeh ___ hai.)

▶ What is that?
  Vo kyā hai? वह क्या है / वो क्या है?
  (Vo kyaa hai?)

▶ What is its price?
  Iskā dām kyā hai? इसका दाम क्या है?
  (Is-kaa daam kyaa hai?)

▶ What did you say?
  Āpné kyā kahā? आपने क्या कहा?
  (Aap-nay kyaa ka-haa?)

▶ What does this mean?
Iskā kyā matlab hai? इसका क्या मतलब है?
(Is-kaa kyaa mut-lub hai?)

▶ When does ___ go / depart?
___ **kab jātā hai?** (for masc. mode, like "plane," "auto,"
"cycle rickshaw" and "truck") /
___ **kab jāti hai?** (for fem. mode, like "bus," "train,"
and "Jeep") ___ कब जाता / जाती है?
(___ kub jaa-taa hai / jaa-tee hai?)

The option to choose here, and for the next two questions,
depends on what mode of transportation you're asking about.
"Plane," "auto," "cycle rickshaw" and "truck" are masculine
in Hindi, while "bus," "train," and "Jeep" are feminine.

▶ When will ___ go / depart?
___ **kab jāyégā?** (for masc. mode) / **jāyégī?** (for fem.
mode) ___ कब जायेगा / जायेगी?
(___ kub jaa-ye-gaa / jaa-ye-gee?)

▶ When did __ leave?
___ **kab gayā?** (for masc. mode) / **gayī?** (for fem. mode)
___ कब गया / गयी?
(___ kub ga-yaa / ga-yee?)

WHERE...? **Kahằ** कहाँ

▶ Where are you from?
  Āp kahằ se hai(n)? आप कहाँ से हैं?
  (Aap ka-haan say hain?)

Many people you meet in India will probably ask you this type of question, simply out of inquisitiveness!

▶ Where are you going?
  Āp kahằ jā rahé hai(n)? आप कहाँ जा रहे हैं?
  (Aap ka-haan jaa ra-hay hain?)

▶ Where do you (all) live?
  Āp sab kahān rehté hain? आप सब कहाँ रहते हैं?
  (Aap sub ka-haan reh-tay hain?)

WHY? **Kyò?** क्यों?

▶ Why?
  Kyò? क्यों?
  (Ky-on?)

▶ Why not?
  Kyò hanĩ? क्यों नहीं?
  (Ky-on na-heen?)

HOW, WHAT, WHO...?

▶ How are you?
  Āp kaisé hai(n)? आप कैसे हैं?
  (Aap kay-say hain?)

► How old are you?
Āp kitné sāl ké hai(n)? आप कितने साल के हैं?
(to ask a male)
(Aap kit-nay saal kay hain?)

Āp kitné sāl kī hai(n)? आप कितने साल की हैं?
(to ask a female)
(Aap kit-nay saal kee hain?)

► How many are there in (it)?
Ismé Kitné hai(n)? इसमें कितने हैं?
(Is-mein kit-nay hain?)

Kitnī hai(n)? कितनी हैं?
(Kit-nee hain?)

Kitnā hai(n)? कितना है?
(Kit-naa hain?)

► How much do you want?
Āpko kitnā chāhiyé? आपको कितना चाहिए?
(Aap-ko kit-naa chaa-he-yay?)

► How do you say this?
Āp isé kaisé kehté haiṅ? आप इसे कैसे कहते हैं?
(Aap is-ay kay-say keh-tay hain?)

► This
Yeh यह
(Yeh)

► What is this?
Yeh kyā hai? यह क्या है?
(Yeh kyaa hai?)

► That
Veh / Vo वह / वो
(Veh / Vo)

► What is that?
Veh kyā hai? वह क्या है?
(Veh kyaa hai?)

► Who is this?
Yeh kaun hai? ये कौन है?
(Yeh kawn hai?)

Who are these? (plural)
Yé kaun hai(n)? ये कौन हैं?
(Yay kawn hain?)

WHICH? **Kaunsā** (m.) / **Kaunsī** (f.) / **Kaunsé** (pl.)

► Which one do you like?
Āpkō kaunsā pasand hai? आपको कौनसा पसंद है?
(Aap-ko kawn-saa pass-und hai?)

► Which way is it?
Yeh Kidhar hai? वो किधर है?
(Yeh kidh-er hai?)

ASKING FOR TOILETS AND RESTROOMS

Public restrooms and toilets in India are not always commonly found, especially in rural areas and smaller cities. Larger metropolitan areas have the government-run bathrooms called "**sulabh shauchalaya**" (literally, "easily available restrooms"). You can find them at railway stations and bus depots. The restrooms in **sulabh shauchalaya** facilities are the "squatter" style. In cities such as Delhi, Mumbai, Jaipur, and Calcutta western-style malls are common, and in them you can find clean western-style restrooms. The bigger tourist monuments usually have good washrooms with western-style toilets. If you face a problem locating any public toilets, you may ask a restaurant or hotel to let you use their toilets. **Advice:** Carry toilet paper, hand sanitizers and hygiene product with you, as they are not commonly available all over India.

► bathroom
  shauchālay शौचालय
  (shaw-chaa-lay)

► Men's restroom
  Purush shauchālay पुरुष शौचालय
  (Pu-ru-sh shaw-chaa-lay)

► Women's restroom
  Mahilā shauchālay महिला शौचालय
  (Ma-hi-laa shaw-chaa-lay)

Since the word "bathroom" is widely used in India for toilets, you can use the word "bathroom" instead of using **shauchālay**:

► Where is the toilet?
Bāthroom kahằ hai? बाथरूम कहाँ है?
(Baa-th room ka-haan hai?)

Shauchālay kahằ hai? शौचालय कहाँ है?
(Shaw-chaa-lay ka-haan hai?)

► Is there any bathroom here?
Yahằ koi bathroom hai? यहाँ कोई बाथरूम है?
(Ya-haan ko-yee baa-th room hai?)

ASKING FOR HELP

Indians in general are very friendly and will be eager to provide you any help. But always use your best judgment and instinct when you ask for help or directions, of course. After all, crooks are found everywhere you go in the world.

► help
madad / sahāytā / help मदद / सहायता / हैल्प
(mud-ud / sa-hai-taa / help)

► hospital
aspatāl / chikitsālay अस्पताल / चिकित्सालय
(us-pa-taal / chi-kit-saa-lay)

► doctor
doctor डॉक्टर
(dock-ter)

▶ police station
pulis thānā / kōtwālī पुलिस थाना / कोतवाली
(pull-is thaa-naa / co-t-waa-lee)

▶ pharmacy
dawāī Khānā दवाईखाना
(da-waa-yee khaa-naa)

▶ Please help me!
Merī madad kījiyé! मेरी मदद कीजिए!
(May-ree mud-ud kee-ji-yay!)

▶ Save me!
Bachāo! बचाओ!
(Bach-aa-o!)

▶ Can you help me?
Kyā āp mérī madad kar sakté hai(n)?
क्या आप मेरी मदद कर सकते हैं?
(Kyaa aap may-ree mud-ud ker suk-tay hain?)

▶ My things got stolen—I need help.
**Mérā sāmān chōrī hō gayā hai, mujhé madad
chāhiyé.**
मेरा सामान चोरी हो गया है, मुझे मदद चाहिए|
*(May-raa saa-maan cho-ree ho ga-yaa hai, mujh-
ay mud-ud chaa-hi-yay.)*

▶ Please, someone help!
Koī mérī madad karo! कोई मेरी मदद करो!
(Ko-ee may-ree mau-ud-ker-o!)

▶ Someone call the police.
Koī pulis kō bulāō. कोई पुलिस को बुलाओ।
(Koee pull-is ko bull-aa-o.)

▶ Call a doctor.
Doktar kō bulāō. डॉक्टर को बुलाओ।
(Dock-ter ko bull-aa-o.)

▶ Call an ambulance.
Ambulance kō bulāō. एम्बुलेंस को बुलाओ।
(Am-bu-lance ko bull-aa-o.)

▶ It's an emergency.
Emergency hai. एमरजैंसी है।
(Emergency hai.)

▶ Is there a police station nearby?
Yahā̃ pās méi(n) koī thānā yā kōtwālī hai?
यहाँ पास में कोई थाना या कोतवाली है?
(Ya-haan paas mein koee pull-is thaa-naa yaa cot-waa-lee hai?)

▶ Is there a hospital nearby?
Yahā̃ pās méi(n) koī aspatāl hai?
यहाँ पास में कोई अस्पताल है?
(Ya-haan paas mein koee us-pa-taal hai?)

PART TWO

Numbers, Time, and Other "Basics"

CARDINAL NUMBERS

1 **ék** एक *(ayk)*	2 **do** दो *(tho)*	3 **tīn** तीन *(teen)*	4 **chār** चार *(chaar)*
5 **pãch** पाँच *(paan-ch)*	6 **Chheh** (छह) *(Chheh)*	7 **sāt** (सात) *(Saat)*	8 **āThh** (आठ) *(Ought)*
9 **nau** (नौ) *(knaw)*	10 **das** (दस) *(thus / dus)*	11 **gyārah** ग्यारह *(gyaa-rah)*	12 **bārah** बारह *(baa-rah)*
13 **térah** (तेरह) *(tey-rah)*	14 **chau-dah** (चौदह) *(chow-dah)*	15 **pandrah** पन्द्रह *(pun-drah)*	16 **solah** सोलह *(soul-ah)*
17 **satrah** सत्रह *(sutt-rah)*	18 **aThhārah** अठारह *(aThhaa-rah)*	19 **unīs** (उन्नीस) *(u-neece)*	20 **bīs** (बीस) *(bees)*
30 **tīs** तीस *(tee-s)*	40 **chālis** चालीस *(chaa-lis)*	50 **pachās** पचास *(puh-ch-aas)*	60 **sāThh** साठ *(saa-Thh)*

70	80	90	100
sattar सत्तर	**assī** अस्सी	**nubbey** नब्बे	**sau** सौ
(sut-ter)	*(us-see)*	*(nub-bay)*	*(saw)*
1000	10,000,000		
ék hazār एक हज़ार	**ék karore** एक करोड़		
(ayk-huzaar)	*(ayk-ker-ore)*		

SANSKRIT ORDINAL NUMBERS

Ordinal Numbers	Transliteration	Pronunciation	Sanskrit
1st	**pratham**	*pr-thum*	प्रथम
2nd	**dwitīya**	*dwi-teeya*	द्वितीय
3rd	**tritīya**	*tri-teeya*	तृतीय
4th	**chatūrth**	*ch-tur-th*	चतुर्थ
5th	**pancham**	*punch-um*	पंचम
6th	**shashTam**	*sh-shT-um*	षष्टम
7th	**saptam**	*supt-um*	सप्तम
8th	**asTham**	*ashT-um*	अष्टम
9th	**navam**	*nuv-um*	नवम
10th	**dasham**	*dush-um*	दशम
11th	**ekādash**	*ayk-aa-dush*	एकादश
12th	**dwādash**	*dwaa-dush*	द्वादश

Ordinal Numbers	Transliteration	Pronunciation	Sanskrit
13th	**trayodash**	*tr-yo-dush*	त्रयोदश
14th	**chaturdash**	*ch-tur-dush*	चतुर्दश

For trains:

▶ First class
pratham shréynī प्रथम श्रेणी
(pr-thum shray-rNee)

▶ Second class
dwitiya shréynī द्वितीय श्रेणी
(dwi-teeyuh shray-rNee)

▶ Third class
tritīya shréynī तृतीय श्रेणी
(tri-teeyuh shray-rNee)

HINDI ORDINAL NUMBERS

▶ First room
peh-lā kamrā पहला कमरा (masculine)

▶ On the first
peh-lee tā-ree-kh ko पहली तारीख़ (feminine)

HINDI ORDINAL NUMBERS

Ordinal Numbers	English Transliteration	Pronunciation	Hindi
1st	**pehlā** (m), **péhlī** (f)	*peh-laa, peh-lee*	पहला, पहली
2nd	**dusrā, dusrī**	*doos-raa, doos-re*	दूसरा, दूसरी
3rd	**tīsrā, tīsrī**	*tees-raa, tees-re*	तीसरा, तीसरी
4th	**chauthā, chauthī**	*chaw-thaa, chaw-thee*	चौथा, चौथी
5th	**pằchvā, pāchvī**	*paan-ch-vaan, paan-ch-veen*	पाँचवाँ, पाँचवीं
6th	**Chha-Thhā, Chha-Thhī**	*Chhuh-TThā, Chhuh-Thhee*	छठा, छठी
7th	**sātvā, sātvī**	*saat-vaan, saat-veen*	सातवाँ, सातवीं
8th	**āThhvằ, āThhvī**	*aaTh-vaan, aaThh-veen*	आठवाँ, आठवीं
9th	**navằ, navī**	*nuv-vaan, nuv-veen*	नवाँ, नवीं
10th	**dasvằ, dasvī**	*dus-vaan, dus-veen*	दसवाँ, दसवीं
11th	**gyārahvhvằ, gyārahvī**	*gyaa-rah-vaan, gyaa-rah-veen*	ग्यारहवाँ, ग्यारहवीं
12th	**bārahvā, bārahvī**	*baa-rah-vaan, baa-rah-veen*	बारहवाँ, बारहवीं

Ordinal Numbers	English Transliteration	Pronunciation	Hindi
13th	**tayrahvằ, tayrahvī**	*tay-rah-vaan, tay-rah-veen*	तेरहवाँ, तेरहवीं
14th	**chaudahvằ, chaudahvī**	*chaw-dah-vaan, chaw-dah-veen*	चौदहवाँ, चौदहवीं
15th	**pandrahvằ, pandrahvī**	*pun-drahh-vaaṅ, pun-drahh-veen*	पन्द्रहवाँ, पन्द्रहवीं

DAYS OF THE WEEK

English	Transliteration	Pronunciation	Hindi
Monday	**Somwār**	*So-m-waar*	सोमवार
Tuesday	**Mangalwār**	*Mung-ul-waar*	मंगलवार
Wednesday	**Budhwār**	*Budh-waar*	बुधवार
Thursday	**Brihaspatiwār, Guruwār**	*Brihas-puti-waar, Guru-waar*	बृहस्पतिवार, गुरुवार
Friday	**Shukrawār**	*Shukruh-waar*	शुक्रवार
Saturday	**Shaniwār**	*Shanee-waar*	शनिवार
Sunday	**Raviwār, Itwār**	*Ravee-wār, It-waar*	रविवार, इतवार

WHICH DAY?

English	Transliteration	Pronunciation	Hindi
today	**āj**	*aaj*	आज
tomorrow / yesterday	**kal**	*kul*	कल
day after tomorrow	**parsò**	*per-sawn*	परसों
two days after tomorrow	**narsò**	*ner-sawn*	नरसों
morning	**subah**	*su-beh*	सुबह
at noon	**din mei(n)**	*din mein*	दिन में
in the afternoon	**dopé har mei(n)**	*tho peh-har mein*	दोपहर में
in the evening	**shām ko**	*shaam ko*	शाम को
at night	**rāt ko**	*raat ko*	रात को
early	**jaldī**	*jul-dee*	जल्दी
late	**dér sé**	*dayr say*	देर से
on / in time	**samay par**	*sum-uy per*	समय पर

MONTHS

As you notice, the names of the months in Hindi are similar to English months. The main difference is in pronunciation.

English	Transliteration	Pronunciation	Hindi
January	**Janvary**	*Jun-vary*	जनवरी
February	**Farvary**	*Ferr-vary*	फ़रवरी
March	**Mārch**	*Maar-ch*	मार्च
April	**Aprail**	*Up-ra-al*	अप्रैल
May	**Mai**	*m-yee*	मई
June	**June**	*June*	जून
July	**Julaī**	*Julaa-ee*	जुलाई
August	**Agust**	*Ug-ust*	अगस्त
September	**Sitamber**	*Sit-umber*	सितम्बर
October	**AcTuber**	*Uck-too-ber*	अक्टूबर
November	**Navamber**	*Nov-umber*	नवम्बर
December	**Disamber**	*Dis-umber*	दिसम्बर

DATES

▶ What is today's date?
Āj kyā tarīkh hai? / Āj kaun sī tarīkh hai?
आज क्या तारीख़ है / आज कौनसी तारीख़ है
(Aaj kyaa taa-reekh hai? / Aaj kawn see taa-reekh hai?)

▶ Today is the 1st of January.
Āj péhlī tarīkh hai. / Āj ék janvary hai. / Āj ék tārikh hai.
आज पहली तारीख है / आज एक जनवरी है / आज एक तारीख़ है|
(Aaj peh-lee jun-vary hai / Aaj ayk jun-vary hai / Aaj ayk taa-reekh hai.)

SEASONS

English	Hindi	Sanskrit	Pronunciation
spring	**basant**	**basant**	*(bus-unt)* बसंत
summer	**garmī**	**grīshm**	*(gur-me / gree-shm)* ग्रीष्म
pre-winter	–	**hémant**	*(hay-munt)* हेमंत
winter	**sardī / sheet**	**shishir**	*(sir-dee / shi-shir)* शिशिर
fall	**patjharD**	**sharad**	*(putt-jhurD / shu-rud)* शरद
rainy	**vershā**	**vershā**	*(ver-shaa)* वर्षा

WEATHER

weather	**mausam**	*(maw-sum)* मौसम
hot	**garm**	*(gurm)* गर्म
cold	**Thhandā**	*(Thun-Daa)* ठंडा
wet	**gīlā**	*(gee-laa)* गीला
rainy	**bārish kā**	*(baa-rish kaa)* बारिश का
humid	**umas**	*(um-us)* उमस
temperature	**tāpmān**	*(taap-maan)* तापमान
maximum	**adhiktam**	*(udhick-tum)* अधिकतम
minimum	**newntam**	*(newn-tum)* न्यूनतम
sky	**āsmān, ākāsh**	*(aas-maan, aak-aash)* आसमान, आकाश
clouds	**bādal**	*(baa-dull)* बादल
rain	**bārish, varshā**	*(baa-rish, ver-shaa)* बारिश / वर्षा
storm	**tufān**	*(too-faan)* तूफ़ान
sand storm	**ādhī, ādharD**	*(aan-dhee, unadh-urD)* आँधी, अंधड़
dry	**sūkhā**	*(soo-khaa)* सूखा
tornado	**chakravāt**	*(chuckr-vaat)* चक्रवात
flood	**bārDh**	*(baa-rDh)* बाढ़
hail	**olé**	*(o-lay)* ओले
earthquake	**bhūkamp**	*(bhoo-kump)* भूकंप

▶ How is the weather today?
  Āj mausam kaisā hai? आज मौसम कैसा है?
  (Aaj maw-sum kai-saa hai?)

► What is today's temperature?
  Āj kā tāpmān kyā hai? आज का तापमान क्या है?
  (Aaj kaa taap-maan kyaa hai?)

► Today the weather is hot.
  Āj mausm garm hai. आज मौसम गर्म है|
  (Aaj-maw-sum gurm hai.)

► Today it's hot.
  Āj garmī hai. आज गर्मी है|
  (Aaj gerr-mee hai.)

► It's sunny today.
  Āj dhūp niklī hai. आज धूप निकली है|
  (Aaj dhoop nick-lee hai.)

► It's going to be cloudy today.
  Āj bādal Chāyé hŏgé. आज बादल छाये होंगे|
  (Aaj baa-dull Chaa-yay hon-gay.)

► It's scorching hot these days.
  **Ājkal bhīsharN garmī parD rahī hai. / Ajkal bahut
  téz garmī parD rahī hai.**
  आजकल भीषण गर्मी पड़ रही है / आजकल बहुत तेज़ गर्मी
  पड़ रही है|
  *(Aaj-kul bhee-shrN gerr-mee perD ruh-ee hai /
  Aaj-kul bahut taze gerr-mee perD ruh-hee hai.)*

► It's very cold today.
  Āj bahut ThàD hai. आज बहुत ठंड है|
  (Aaj-bahut ThunD hai.)

- It's going to rain today.
  Āj bārish hōgī. आज बारिश होगी|
  (Aaj baa-rish ho-gee.)

- It's raining.
  Bārish ho rahī hai. बारिश हो रही है|
  (Baa-rish ho-ruh-ee hai.)

- It's very pleasant today.
  Āj mausam bahut suhānā hai.
  आज मौसम बहुत सुहाना है|
  (Aaj maw-sum bahut su-haa-naa hai.)

ASKING AND TELLING TIME

- What time is it?
  Kitné bajé hai(n)? कितने बजे हैं?
  (Kit-nay buj-ay hain?)

  Kyā bajā hai? क्या बजा है?
  (Kyaa buj-aa hai?)

Note: When asking a stranger for the time, if it's a man always ask formally and politely, "*Bhai sahib, kit-ne buj-ay hain?*" When asking a woman, ask "*Behen ji kitnay buj-aa hain?*"

  Kyā vaqt huā hai? क्या वक़्त हुआ है?
  (Kyaa vu-qut hu-aa hai?)

  Kyā Time huā hai? क्या टाइम हुआ है?
  (Kyaa time huaa hai?)

A reminder: Wherever the letter "n" is in parentheses, read it at the end of the previous letter as a nasal sound—as if you are producing the sound from your nose.

▶ 1:00 **ék bajā hai.** एक बजा है।
(ayk buj-aa hai)

▶ 2:00 **do bajé hai(n).** दो बजे हैं।
(tho buj-a hain)

▶ 3:00 **tīn bajé hai(n).** तीन बजे हैं।
(teen buj-a hain)

▶ 4:00 **chār bajé hai(n).** चार बजे हैं।
(chaar buj-a hain)

▶ 5:00 **păch bajé hai(n).** पाँच बजे हैं।
(paan-ch buj-a hain)

▶ 6:00 **Chheh bajé hai(n).** छह बजे हैं।
(Chheh buj-a hain)

▶ 7:00 **sāt bajé hai(n).** सात बजे हैं।
(saat buj-a hain)

▶ 8:00 **āThh bajé hai(n).** आठ बजे हैं।
(aa-Thh buj-a hain)

▶ 9:00 **nau bajé hai(n)** नौ बजे हैं।
(knaw buj-a hain)

▶ 10:00 **das bajé hai(n).** दस बजे हैं।
(dus buj-a hain)

▶ 11:00 **gyārah bajé hai(n).** ग्यारह बजे हैं।
(gyaa-rah buj-a hain)

▶ 12:00 **bārah bajé hai(n).** बारह बजे हैं।
(baa-rah buhj-a hain)

▶ 12:15 **savā bārah bajé hai(n).** सवा बारह बजे हैं।
(suv-aa baarh buj-a hain)

▶ 1:15 **savā bajé hai(n).** सवा बजे हैं।
(suv-aa buj-a hain)

- ▶ 2:15   **savā do bajé hai(n).** सवा दो बजे हैं।
  (suv-aa tho buj-a hain)
- ▶ 3:15   **savā tīn bajé hai(n).** सवा तीन बजे हैं।
  (suv-aa teen buj-a hain)
- ▶ 4:15   **savā chār bajé hai(n).** सवा चार बजे हैं।
  (suv-aa chaar buj-a hain)
- ▶ 5:15   **savā păch bajé hai(n).** सवा पाँच बजे हैं।
  (suv-aa paan-ch buj-a hain)
- ▶ 6:15   **savā Chheh bajé hai(n).** सवा छह बजे हैं।
  (suv-aa Chheh buj-a hain)
- ▶ 7:15   **savā sāt bajé hai(n).** सवा सात बजे हैं।
  (suv-aa saat buj-a hain)
- ▶ 8:15   **savā āThh bajé hai(n).** सवा आठ बजे हैं।
  (suv-aa aa-Thh buj-a hain)
- ▶ 9:15   **savā nau bajé hai(n).** सवा नौ बजे हैं।
  (suv-aa knaw buj-a hain)
- ▶ 10:15   **savā dus bajé hai(n).** सवा दस बजे हैं।
  (suv-aa dus buj-a hain)
- ▶ 11:15   **savā gyārah bajé hai(n).** सवा ग्यारह बजे हैं।
  (suv-aa gyaa-rah buj-a hain)
- ▶ 12:30   **sārDhé bārah bajé hai(n).** साढ़े बारह बजे हैं।
  (saa-rDh-a baa-rah buj-a hain)
- ▶ 1:30   **Dérah bajé hai(n).** डेढ़ बजे हैं।
  (Day-rDh buj-a hain)
- ▶ 2:30   **Dhāi bajé hai(n).** ढाई बजे हैं।
  (Dhaa-ee buj-a hain)
- ▶ 3:30   **sārDhé tin bajé hai(n).** साढ़े तीन बजे हैं।
  (saa-rDh-a teen buj-a hain)
- ▶ 4:30   **sārDhé chār bajé hai(n).** साढ़े चार बजे हैं।
  (saa-rDh-a chaar buj-a hain)
- ▶ 5:30   **sārDhé păch bajé hai(n).** साढ़े पाँच बजे हैं।
  (saa-rDh-a paanch buj-a hain)

▶ 6:30   **sārDhé Chheh bajé hai(n).** साढ़े छह बजे हैं‌।
(saa-rDh-a Chheh buj-a hain)

▶ 7:30   **sārDhé sāt bajé hai(n).** साढ़े सात बजे हैं‌।
(saa-rDh-a saat buj-a hain)

▶ 8:30   **sārDhé āThh bajé hai(n).** साढ़े आठ बजे हैं‌।
(saa-rDh-a aa-Thh buj-a hain)

▶ 9:30   **sārDhé nau bajé hai(n).** साढ़े नौ बजे हैं‌।
(saa-rDh-a knaw buj-a hain)

▶ 10:30   **sārDhé das bajé hai(n).** साढ़े दस बजे हैं‌।
(saa-rDh-a dus buj-a hain)

▶ 11:30   **sārDhé gyārah bajé hai(n).** साढ़े ग्यारह बजे हैं‌।
(saa-rDh-a gyaa-rah buj-a hain)

▶ 11:45   **pauné bārah bajé hai(n).** पौने बारह बजे हैं‌।
(pawn-a baa-rah buj-a hain)

▶ 1:45   **pauné do bajé hai(n).** पौने दो बजे हैं‌।
(pawn-a tho buj-a hain)

▶ 2:45   **pauné tīn bajé hai(n).** पौने तीन बजे हैं‌।
(pawn-a teen buj-a hain)

▶ 3:45   **pauné chār bajé hai(n).** पौने चार बजे हैं‌।
(pawn-a chaar buj-a hain)

▶ 4:45   **pauné pā̃ch bajé hai(n).** पौने पाँच बजे हैं‌।
(pawn-a paanch buj-a hain)

▶ 5:45   **pauné Chheh bajé hai(n).** पौने छह बजे हैं‌।
(pawn-a Chheh buj-a hain)

▶ 6:45   **pauné sāt bajé hai(n).** पौने सात बजे हैं‌।
(pawn-a saat buj-a hain)

▶ 7:45   **pauné āThh bajé hai(n).** पौने आठ बजे हैं‌।
(pawn-a aa-Thh buj-a hain)

▶ 8:45   **pauné nau bajé hai(n).** पौने नौ बजे हैं‌।
(pawn-a knaw buj-a hain)

▶ 9:45 **pauné das bajé hai(n).** पौने दस बजे हैं।
   (pawn-a dus buj-a hain)
▶ 10:45 **pauné gyārah bajé hai(n).** पौने ग्यारह बजे हैं।
   (pawn-a gyaa-rah buj-a hain)

After = X hour + **bajkar** + Y minute

▶ 1:05 five minutes after one
   ék bajkar pā̃ch minuTe एक बजकर पाँच मिनट
   (ayk buj-ker paan-ch-min-uT)

▶ 2:10 ten minutes after two
   do bajkar das minuTe दो बजकर दस मिनट
   (tho buj-ker dus min-uT)

Before = X hour + **bajné mein** + Y minute

▶ 10:50 ten minutes to eleven
   gyārah bajné mei(n) das minuTe
   ग्यारह बजने में दस मिनट
   (Gyaa-rah buj-nay mein dus min-uT)

▶ 9:40 twenty minutes to ten
   das bajné mei(n) bīs minute दस बजने में बीस मिनट
   (dus buj-nay mein bees min-ut)

TIMES IN A DAY

morning	**subah** सुबह	*(su-beh)*
noon	**din** दिन	*(din)*
afternoon	**do péhar** दोपहर	*(tho-peh-er)*
evening	**shām** शाम	*(shaam)*
in the morning	**subah** सुबह	*(su-beh)*
at noon	**din mei(n)** दिन में	*(din meiṅ)*
in the afternoon	**do péhar mei(n)** दोपहर में	*(though-peh-er mein)*
in the evening	**shām ko** शाम को	*(sham ko)*
at night	**rāt ko** रात को	*(raat ko)*

To indicate the times of the day with hour:

▶ Ten o'clock in the morning
 subah ké das bajé सुबह के दस बजे
 (su-beh kay dus buj-a)

▶ Twelve o'clock at noon
 din ké bārah bajé दिन के बारह बजे
 (din kay baa-rah buj-a)

▶ Three o'clock in the afternoon
 do péhar ké tīn bajé दोपहर के तीन बजे
 (tho puh-er ke teen buj-a)

- ▶ Five o'clock in the evening
  shām ké pǎch bajé शाम के पाँच बजे
  (sham kay paan-ch buj-a)

- ▶ Eight o'clock at night
  rāt ké āThh bajé रात के आठ बजे
  (raat kay aa-Thh buj-a)

FAMILY

English	Transliteration	Pronunciation	Hindi
Paternal Grandfather	**dādā**	*daa-daa*	दादा
Paternal Grandmother	**dādī**	*daa-dee*	दादी
Maternal Grandfather	**nānā**	*naa-naa*	नाना
Maternal Grandmother	**nānī**	*naa-nee*	नानी
Father	**pitā-jī, pā-pā, bā-pū**	*pit-a-jee, paa-paa, baa-poo*	पिता जी, पापा, बापू
Mother	**mātā-jī, mǎ, mummy**	*maa-taa-jee, maa-n, mummy*	माता जी, माँ, मम्मी

English	Transliteration	Pronunciation	Hindi
Brother	**bhāī, bhaiyā** (older brother)	*bha-ee, bhuh-ee-yaa*	भाई, भइया
Brother's Wife	**bhābhī**	*bhaa-bhee*	भाभी
Sister	**béhén**	*be-hen*	बहन
Sister's Husband	**behnōi, ji-jā-jī**	*beh-no-ee, jee-jaa-jee*	बहनोई, जीजा जी
Husband	**pati**	*putt-ee*	पति
Wife	**patni**	*putt-nee*	पत्नि
Children	**bachché**	*buh-ch-a*	बच्चे
Son	**béTā**	*bay-Taa*	बेटा
Daughter	**béTī**	*bay-Tee*	बेटी
Father's Older Brother	**tāujī**	*taa-oo-jee*	ताऊ जी
Wife of Father's Older Brother	**taījī**	*taa-ee-jee*	ताई जी
Father's Younger Brother	**chāchā jī**	*chaa-chaa-jee*	चाचा जी
Wife of Father's Younger Brother	**chāchi jī**	*chaa-chee-jee*	चाची जी
Mother's Brother	**māmā jī**	*maa-maa-jee*	मामा जी

English	Transliteration	Pronunciation	Hindi
Wife of Mother's Brother	**māmi jī**	*maa-me-jee*	मामी जी
Mother's Sister	**mausī**	*maw-see*	मौसी
Husband of Mother's Sister	**mausā jī**	*maw-saa-jee*	मौसा जी
Nephew (brother's son)	**bhatījā**	*bh-tea-jaa*	भतीजा
Nephew (sister's son)	**bhānjā**	*bhaa-n-jaa*	भानजा
Niece (brother's daughter)	**bhatījī**	*bh-tee-jee*	भतीजी
Niece (sister's daughter)	**bhānjī**	*bhaa-n-jee*	भानजी

PARTS OF THE BODY

English	Transliteration	Pronunciation	Hindi
head	**sir**	*si-r*	सिर
hair	**bāl**	*baal*	बाल
ear/s	**kān**	*kaan*	कान
eye	**ånkh**	*aan-kh*	आँख
eyes	**ånkhé(n)**	*aan-khein*	आँखें
cheek/s	**gāl**	*gaal*	गाल

English	Transliteration	Pronunciation	Hindi
mouth	**mů̃h**	*moon-h*	मुँह
tooth / teeth	**dā̃t**	*daant*	दाँत
lip/s	**hõ̇Th**	*hon-Thh*	होंठ
nose	**nāk**	*naa-k*	नाक
shoulder	**kȧdhā**	*kun-dhaa*	कंधा
shoulders	**kȧdhé**	*kun-dh-a*	कंधे
chest	**Chātī**	*Chh-aa-tea*	छाती
back	**pīTh**	*pee-Thh*	पीठ
stomach	**péT**	*pay-T*	पेट
waist	**kamar**	*kum-er*	कमर
hand/s	**hāth**	*haa-th*	हाथ
wrist	**kalāi**	*kul-aa-ee*	कलाई
finger	**anguli / unglī**	*ung-oo-lee / oong-lee*	अँगुली / उँगली
fingers	**ȧgu-liyȧ̃ / ung-liyȧ̃**	*ung-u-lee-yaan / oong-lee-yaan*	अँगुलियाँ / उँगलियाँ
thumb	**ȧgūThā**	*ung-oo-Thhaa*	अँगूठा
thumbs	**ȧgūThé**	*Ung-oo-Thh-a*	अँगूठे
leg	**Tȧg**	*Taa-ng*	टाँग
legs	**Tȧ-gé(n)**	*Taa-ng-ein*	टाँगें
foot	**pér**	*pa-r*	पैर

English	Transliteration	Pronunciation	Hindi
skin	**cham-rDī**	*chum-rDee*	चमड़ी
nail/s	**nākhūn**	*naa-khoon*	नाख़ून
knee	**ghuTnā**	*ghu-T-naa*	घुटना
knees	**ghuTné**	*ghu-T-nay*	घुटने
hip	**cūlhā**	*cool-haa*	कूल्हा
hips	**culhé**	*cool-hey*	कूल्हे
heel	**érDhī**	*a-rDh-ee*	एड़ी
heels	**érDhiyằ**	*a-rDh-i-yaan*	एड़ियाँ

MAP DIRECTIONS

▶ North
  Uttar उत्तर
  (ut-ter)

▶ South
  Dakshin दक्षिण
  (duk-shirN)

▶ East
  Pūrv / Pūrab पूर्व / पूरब
  (poo-rv / poo-rub)

▶ West
  Pashchim पश्चिम
  (puh-sh-chim)

PART THREE

Getting Around

AT THE AIRPORT

India offers many interstate airlines, and travel has become easier for foreign as well as Indian travelers. There are many good services available for most of the larger metropolitan areas in India.

airport	**hawāi aDDā** हवाई अड्डा
	(huwaa-ee uDD-aa)
airplane	**hawāī jahāz** हवाईजहाज़
	(huwaa-ee juhaaz)
first class	**pratham shrénī** प्रथम श्रेणी
	(pr-thum-shrey-nee)
one way	**ék tarfā** एक तरफ़ा
	(ayk terf-aa)
round trip	**ānā-jānā** आना-जाना
	(aa-naa- jaa-naa)
flight	**urDān** उड़ान
	(u-rDaan)
flight number	**urDān sankhyā** उड़ान संख्या
	(oo-rDaan sunkh-yaa)

"Business," "economy," "check-in" and "connecting flights" are said with the English words.

reservation	**ārakshan** आरक्षण *(aa-ruk-shun)*
baggage	**sāmān** सामान *(saa-maan)*
aisle seat	**galīyāré wālī seat** गलियारे वाली सीट *(gulee-yaa-ray waa-lee seat)*
window seat	**khirDkī wālī seat** खिड़की वाली सीट *(khirD-kee waa-lee seat)*
boarding time	**chrDhné kā samay** चढ़ने का समय *(chu-rDh-nay kaa sum-ay)*
departure time	**ChūTné / prasthān kā samay** छूटने / प्रस्थान का समय *(chooT-nay kaa sum-ay)*
arrival time	**āné / āgman kā samay** आने / आगमन का समय *(aa-gum-un kaa sum-ay)*
attention please	**kripyā dhyān dījīyé** कृपया ध्यान दीजिए *(krip-a-yaa dhyaa-n-dee-ji-yay)*
departing flight	**jāné wālī urDān** जाने वाली उड़ान *(jaa-nay waa-lee urD-aan)*
arriving flight	**āné wālī urDān** आने वाली उड़ान *(aa-nay waa-lee urD-aan)*
gate number	**dwār sankhyā** द्वार संख्या *(dwaar sunkh-yaa)*
security check	**surakshā jāch** सुरक्षा जाँच *(sur-uk-shaa jaan-ch)*
information	**jānkārī** जानकारी *(jaan-kaa-ree)*
passenger	**yātrī/yātrīgarN** यात्री / यात्रीगण *(yaat-ree / yaat-re-ga-rN)*

▶ I would like an aisle seat.
Mujhé galiyāray wālī seat chāhiyé.
मुझे गलियारे वाली सीट चाहिए|
(Mujh-ay guli-yaa-ray waa-lee seat chaa-hi-yay.)

▶ I would like a window seat.
Mujhé khirDkī wāli seat chāhiyé.
मुझे खिड़की वाली सीट चाहिए|
(Mujh-ay khi-rD-kee waa-lee seat chaa-hi-yay.)

▶ I need to go to the airport.
Mujhé hawāī aDDé jānā hai.
मुझे हवाई अड्डे जाना है|
(Mujh-ay huwaa-ee aDD-ay jaa-naa hai.)

HIRING A TAXI OR AUTORICKSHAW

Taxis and autorickshaws are the primary modes of road transportation in India. They both run on meters. Taxis can be hired for longer-distance transportation, but autorick-shaws are used for transportation within a city. Taxis are mainly painted black and yellow and can be easily located. Auto-rickshaws are painted green and yellow.

▶ fare
bhārDā, kirāyā भाड़ा, किराया
(bhaa-rDaa, kir-aa-yaa)

▶ I need a taxi.
Mujhé ék taxi chāhiyé. मुझे एक टैक्सी चाहिए|
(Mujh-ay ayk taxi chaa-he-yay.)

▶ Will you go to ___ ?
  ___ chalōgé? चलोगे?
  (___ ch-low-gay?)

▶ Is this taxi available?
  Kyā yéh taxi khālī hai? क्या यह टैक्सी खाली है?
  (Kyaa yeh taxi khaa-lee hai?)

▶ Let's go.
  Chaliyé. चलिए|
  (ch-li-yay.)

▶ How much will you charge for going to ___ ?
  ___ jāné kā kitnā lōgé / léngé?
  ___ जाने का कितना लोगे / कितना लेंगे?
  (___ jaa-nay kaa kit-naa lo-gay / kit-naa len-gay?)

▶ How much is it to go to ___ ?
  ___ jāné méin kitné lagéngé? ___ जाने में कितने लगेंगे?
  (___ jaa-nay main kit-nay lug-an-gay?)

▶ Is your meter on?
  Kyā tumhārā / apkā meter chālū hai?
  क्या तुम्हारा / आपका मीटर चालू है?
  (Kyaa tu-m-haa-raa / aap-kaa meter chaa-loo hai?)

▶ How far is this place?
  Yeh jagah kitnī dur hai? यह जगह कितनी दूर है?
  (yeh jug-ah kit-nee doo-r hai?)

► Can you please wait for few minutes?
Kyā āp thōdī dér intzār kar sakté hai(n)?
क्या आप थोड़ी देर इंतज़ार कर सकते हैं?
(Kyaa aap tho-rDee day-r int-zar ker suk-tay hain?)

► I will be right back.
Mai(n) abhī ātā hǔ. / Mai(n) abhī āyā. (m. spkr)
मैं अभी आता हूँ / मैं अभी आया।
(Main abhee aa-taa hoon / Main abhee aa-yaa.)

► I will be right back.
Mai(n) abhī ātī hǔ / Mai(n) abhī āyī. (f. spkr)
मैं अभी आती हूँ / मैं अभी आयी।
(Main abhee aa-tee hoon / Main abhee aa-yee.)

► Please slow down.
Dhīré chaliyé. धीरे चलिए।
(dhee-ray ch-lee-yay.)

► Please drive slowly.
thorDā dhīré chalāiyé. थोड़ा धीरे चलाइए।
(tho-rDaa dhee-ray chal-aa-i-yay.)

► Please stop.
Zarā rukiyé. ज़रा रुकिए।
(Za-raa ru-ki-yay.)

► How much do I owe you?
Mujhé tumhén / āpko kitné déné hai(n)?
मुझे तुम्हें / आपको कितने देने हैं?
(Mujh-ay tum-hein / aap-ko kit-nay day-nay hain?)

RENTING A VEHICLE

car	**gārDī** गाड़ी	
	(gaa-rDee)	
driver	**chālak** चालक	
	(chaa-luck)	
air conditioned	**vātānukūlit** वातानुकूलित	
	(vaa-taa-nook-oo-lit)	
speed limit	**gatī sīmā** गति सीमा	
	(gut-ee seem-aa)	
in the morning	**subah** सुबह	
	(su-beh)	
right now	**abhī** अभी	
	(abh-ee)	
at midnight	**ādhī rāt kō** आधी रात को	
	(aa-dhee raat ko)	

▶ I need to rent a car.
Mujhé kirāyé par ék gārDī chāhiyé.
मुझे किराये पर एक गाड़ी चाहिए|
(Mujh ay kiraa-yay per ayk gaa-rDee chaa-hi-yay.)

▶ I also need a driver.
Mujhé ék driver / chālak bhī chāhiyé.
मुझे एक ड्राइवर / चालक भी चाहिए|
(Mujh ayk driver / chaa-luck bh-ee chaa-hi-yay.)

▶ How much is it by the day?
Har din kā kitnā lagégā? हर दिन का कितना लगेगा?
(Her din kaa kit-naa lag-ay-gaa?)

▶ I need it for ___ days.
Mujhé ___ din ké liyé chāhiyé.
मुझे __ दिन के लिए चाहिए|
(Mujh-ay ___ din kay le-yay chaa-he-yay.)

▶ I need an air-conditioned car.
Mujhé ék air-conditioned car chāhiyé.
मुझे एक एयर कंडीशंड कार चाहिए|
(Mujh-ay ayk airconditioned car chaa-he-yay.)

▶ I need the car for a week / ten days.
Mujhé car ék hafté / das dinó ké liyé cháhiyé.
मुझे कार एक हफ़्ते / दस दिनों के लिए चाहिए|
(Mujh-ay car ayk huft-ay / dus din-on kay lee-yay chaa-he-yay.)

▶ How much is it for ten days?
Das dinó kā kitnā kirāyā lagégā?
दस दिनों का कितना किराया लगेगा?
(dus din-on kaa kit-naa kir-aayaa lag-ay-gaa?)

▶ Does it include insurance and mileage?
Ismein bima aur duri bhi shamil hai?
क्या इसमें बीमा और दूरी भी शामिल है?
(Is-mein bee-maa aur doo-ree bhi shaa-mil hai?)

▶ I need the car at 10:00.
Mujhé das baje car chāhiyé. मुझे दस बजे कार चाहिए|
(Mujh-ay dus buj-ay car chaa-he-yay.)

HIRING A CYCLE RICKSHAW

Cycle rickshaws can be seen everywhere you go in India. They are pedal-powered, by a human being! When calling a rickshaw, say "Hey rick-shay waa-lay-jee" or "Hey rick-shaw."

▶ Will you go to ___?
   ___ chalōgé? ___ चलोगे?
   (___ ch-lo-gay?)

▶ Is this rickshaw available?
   Kyā yéh rickshaw khālī hai? क्या यह रिक्शा खाली है?
   (Kyaa yeh rick-shaw khaa-lee hai?)

▶ I need to go to ___.
   Mujhé ___ jānā hai. मुझे ___ जाना है|
   (Mujh-ay ___ jaa-naa hai.)

AT A TRAIN STATION

The primary mode of traveling from one end of India to the other is by train. If you really want to experience the hustle-bustle and diverse colors of India, then trains are the way to go. Before you board a train make sure you have your seat or berth reserved, which is done electronically.

train	**railgārDī** रेलगाड़ी
	(rail-gaa-rDee)
passenger train	**passaenger gārDī** पैसेंजर गाड़ी
	(passenger gaa-rDee)

express train	**express gārDī** एक्सप्रैस गाड़ी
	(express gaa-rDee)

A passenger train is a slow train that makes multiple stops.
It is convenient for getting on and off at small towns and
villages.

Ticket Window	**tikat khirdkī** टिकट खिड़की
	(tick-ut khi-rDkee)
Ticket Office	**tikat ghar** टिकट घर
	(tick-ut ghar)
	tickat kāryālay टिकट कार्यालय
	(tick-ut kar-yaa-lay)
Inquiry	**pūChhtāChh** पूछताछ
	(poo-Chh-taa-Chh)
Information	**jānkārī** जानकारी
	(jaan-kaa-ree)
reservation	**ārakshan** आरक्षण
	(aa-ruck-shun)
First Class	**pratham shrénī** प्रथम श्रेणी
	(pr-thum shrey-nee)
Second Class	**dwitīy shrénī** द्वितीय श्रेणी
	(dwi-teey shrey-nee)
Third Class	**tritīy shrénī** तृतीय श्रेणी
	(tri-tee-y shre-nee)
Sleeper Coach	**shayan yān** शयन यान
	(sh-yun yaan)
Chair Car	**kursī yān** कुर्सी यान
	(kur-see yaan)
Dining Car	**bhōjan yān** भोजन यान
	(bho-jun yaan)

AC Three Tier	**vātānukūlit three teir** वातानुकूलित थ्री टियर *(vaa-taa-nu-cool-it three tiers)*
Compartment	**cūpā** कूपा *(coo-paa)*
Waiting Area	**pratīkhshālay** प्रतीक्षालय *(pr-teek-shaa-lay)*
Rest Area	**vishrāmālay** विश्रामालय *(vishraam-aa-lay)*
Cafeteria	**bhōjnālay** भोजनालय *(bhoj-naa-lay)*
Toilets	**shauchālay** शौचालय *(shau-chaa-lay)*
Complaints	**shikāyat** शिकायत *(shi-kaa-yut)*
Reserved Seat	**ārakshit seat** आरक्षित सीट *(aa-ruck-shi-t seat)*
Unreserved Seat	**anārakshit seat** अनारक्षित सीट *(un-aa-ruck-shi-t seat)*
Get on board	**train par chrDhnā** ट्रेन पर चढ़ना *(train per ch-rDh-naa)*
Get off train	**train se utarnā** ट्रेन से उतरना *(train say ut-er-naa)*
Station Superintendent	**station adhīkshak** स्टेशन अधीक्षक *(stay-tion adh-eek-shuck)*
Station Master	**Station Master** स्टेशन मास्टर *(stay-tion maas-ter)*
Ticket Collector	**T.T** टी.टी *(tee-tee)*
Departure	**prasthān** प्रस्थान *(pr-us-thaan)*

Arrival	**āgman** आगमन
	(aag-mun)
departing train	**jāné wālī gādī** जाने वाली गाड़ी
	(jaa-nay waa-lee gaa-rDee)
arriving train	**āné wālī gādī** आनेवाली गाड़ी
	(aa-nay waa-lee gaa-rDee)

▶ The train coming from ___ is expected to arrive 30 minutes late.

___ sé āné wāli gādī ādhā ghantā dérī sé āné kī sambhāvnā hai. ___ से आने वाली गाड़ी आधा घंटा देरी से आने की संभावना है|

(___ say aa-nay waa-lee gaa-rDee aa-dhaa ghun-taa day-re say aa-nay key sum-bhaav-naa hai.)

▶ The train arriving from ___ is coming on platform number ___.

___ sé āné wālī gārDī platform number ___ par ā rahī hai. ___ से आने वाली गाड़ी प्लेटफॉर्म नम्बर __ पर आ रही है|

(___ say aa-nay waa-lee gaa-rDee plat-form number ___ per aa rahee hai.)

▶ Where is the ticket office?
Tickat ghar kahā̃ hai? टिकट घर कहाँ है?
(Tick-ut gh-er ka-haan hai?)

▶ I need two tickets for Jaipur.
Mujhé Jaipur ké liyé do ticket chāhiyé.
मुझे जयपुर के लिए दो टिकट चाहिए|
(Mujh-ay Jai-pur kay li-yay tho Tick-ut chaa-hi-yay.)

► I need to buy an Indian rail pass, whom should I see?

Mujhé Indian rail pāss khrīdnā hai, mai(n) kis sé milū? मुझे इंडियन रेल पास खरीदना है मैं किस से मिलूँ?

(Mujh-ay Indian rail pass kh-reed-naa hai, main kiss-say mill-oon?)

► Do you have space in "foreign tourists quota"?

Kyā āpké pās foreign tourist quoté mei(n) jagah khālī hai?

क्या आपके पास फ़ॉरिन टूरिस्ट कोटे में जगह खाली है?

(Kyaa aap-kay paas foreign tourists quote mein jug-ah hai?)

As its name suggests, a separate "foreign tourist quota" has been provided for the convenience of foreign nationals, in all classes and in nearly all trains. International tourists holding valid passports can also obtain Indian railpasses using payment in U.S. Dollars, Pounds, Sterling, Euros and Indian Rupees from any reservation office.

► Can I get two tickets in "tatkal quota"?

Kyā mujhé tatkāl quoté mei(n) dō ticket mil sakté hain?

क्या मुझे तत्काल कोटे में दो टिकट मिल सकते हैं?

(Kyaa mujh-ay tat-kaal mein tho tick-ut mill suk-tay hain?)

Tatkal in English means "immediate," and it is an emergency reservation program. You may buy "tatkal quota" tickets a few days before your departure.

METRO RAIL

In major cities in India, such as Delhi, Mumbai, Chennai, Banglore and Hydrabad, the metro is a very convenient way to travel, and to avoid traffic. Metro rail service in India is fully automated. The metro lines run till 11 p.m.

▶ Where is the metro rail station?
Yahā̃ metro rail station kahā̃ hai?
यहाँ मैट्रो रेल स्टेशन कहाँ है?
(Ya-haan miet-row rail station ka- haan hai?)

▶ Can I get a metro rail guide in English?
Kyā mujhé metro rail guide angrezī mein dé sakté hain? क्या मुझे मैट्रो रेल गाइड अंग्रेज़ी में दे सकते हैं?
(Kyaa mujh-ay met-row rail gaa-ide ung-ray-zee mein day suk-tay hain?)

▶ Where can I get off to go to___?
___ jāné ké liyé mai(n) kaunsé station par utrū̃?
___ जाने के लिए मैं कौनसे स्टेशन पर उतरूँ?
(___ jaa-nay kay li-yay main kawn-say station per ut-roon?)

▶ How often does the metro run?
Metrō kitnī-kitnī dér mein jāti hai?
मैट्रो कितनी-कितनी देर में जाती है?
(Met-row kit-nee kit-nee day-r mein jaa-tee hai?)

▶ What color line goes to ___?
___ ké liyé kaunsé rang kī line jātī hai?
___ के लिए कौनसे रंग की लाइन जाती है?
(___ Kay lee-yay kawn-say rung kee line jaa-tee hai?)

TRAVELING BY BUS

Since all the cities are interconnected through a state-run bus network, traveling by bus is a very common and cost effective method of transportation in India. Every city has its own bus depot or bus stand where you can buy tickets. Traveling like a local has its challenges—sometimes you will find the bus crammed with people—yet can be highly enjoyable!

bus station	**bus aDDā** बस अड्डा *(bus uD-Daa)*
state roadways	**rajya path parivahan nigam** राज्य पथ परिवहन निगम *(raaj-ya pa-th pari-va-hun ni-gum)*
interstate bus station	**antar rājiy bus aDDā** अंतर्राज्यीय बस अड्डा *(un-ter-raa-jeey bus aD-Daa)*

▶ How much is the fare to ___?
___ ke liye kiraya kitna hai?
___ के लिए किराया कितना है?
(___ kay le-yay kiraa-yaa kit-naa hai?)

▶ Where is the bus station?
Bus aDDā kidhar hai? बस अड्डा किधर है?
(Bus uD-Daa ki-dher hai?)

▶ When does the bus to ___ leave?
___ jāné wālī bus kitné bajé jātī hai?
___ जाने वाली बस कितने बजे जाती है?
(___ jaa-nay waa-lee bus kit-nay buj-ay jaa-tee hai?)

▶ Does this bus stop in ___?
Kyā yé bus ___ mei(n) ruktī hai?
क्या ये बस ___ में रुकती है?
(Kyaa ye bus ___ mein ruk-tee hai?)

▶ I have to get off at ___.
Mujhé ___mein utarnā hai. मुझे ___ में उतरना है|
(Mujh-ay ___ mein ut-er-naa hai.)

▶ Which city is this?
Yé kaunsā shahar hai? ये कौनसा शहर है?
(Yay kawn-saa sha-har hai?)

▶ What is the next bus stop?
Aglā bus stop kaunsa hai? अगला बस स्टॉप कौनसा है?
(Ug-laa bus stop kawn-saa hai?)

ASKING FOR DIRECTIONS & LOCATIONS

direction	**dishā** दिशा
	(dish-aa)
toward	**… kī taraf / … kī ore** की तरफ़ / … की ओर
	(… kee ter-uf / … kee ore)
straight	**sīdhé** सीधे
	(see-dhay)
left	**bāyé / bāyī** बायें / बायीं
	(baa-yen / baa-yeen)
to the left	**bāyī taraf** बायीं तरफ़
	(baa-yeen ter-uf)
right	**dāyé / dāyī** दायें / दायीं
	(daa-yen / daa-yeen)

to the right	**dāyī taraf** दायीं तरफ़
	(daa-yeen ter-uf)
across	**pār / us pār / ... ké us pār**
	पार / उस पार / ...के उस पार
	(paar / us paar / ... kay us paar)
behind	**pīChhé** पीछे
	(pee-Chh-ay)
behind it	**... ké pīChhé** ...के पीछे
	(... kay pee-Chh-ay)
there	**vahăं** वहाँ
	(va-haan)
here	**yahăं** यहाँ
	(ya-haan)
near	**... ké pās** ...के पास
	(... kay paas)
nearby	**... ké ās-pās** ... के आस-पास
	(...kay aas-paas)
how many miles?	**kitné mīl?** कितने मील?
	(kit-nay meel)
how many kilometers?	**kitné kilometer hai?** कितने किलोमीटर है?
	(kit-nay ki-lo-mee-ter hai?)
how far is it?	**... kitnī dūr hai?** ... कितनी दूर है?
	(... kit-nee door hai?)
opposite of	**... ké sāmné** के सामने
	(... kay saam-nay)
neighborhood	**parDos** पड़ोस
	(perD-os)
in the neighborhood	**parDos mei(n)** पड़ोस में
	(perD-os mein)
walking distance	**pās hī mei(n)** पास ही में
	(pass-hee mein)

▶ As soon as the road ends
  SarDak khatm hoté hī सड़क खत्म होते ही|
  (SerDak khatum ho-tay hi)

▶ At this intersection
  Is chaurāhé par इस चौराहे पर
  (Is chaw-raa-hay per)

▶ On the fourth floor
  Chauthī manzil par चौथी मंज़िल पर
  (chaw-thee mun-zil per)

India follows the British system of labeling floors. In contrast to the American system, in India the ground floor is called just that, not the "first" floor. "G+4 floor" means a building has 5 stories.

▶ It is just around the corner.
  Yahī pās hī mei(n) hai. यहीं पास ही में है|
  (Ya-heen paas hee mein hai.)

▶ I'm looking for this place.
  Mai(n) yeh jagah DhūnDh rahā hŭ
  मैं यह जगह ढूँढ रहा हूँ| (m. spkr)
  (Main yeh jagah Dhhoo-nDhh raha hoon.)

  Mai(n) yeh jagah DhūnDh rahī hŭ
  मैं यह जगह ढूँढ रही हूँ| (f. spkr)
  (main yeh jagah Dhhoo-nDhh ra-hee hoon.)

▶ Where is this place?
  Yé jagah kahā hai? ये जगह कहाँ है?
  (Ye jug-ah ka-haan hai?)

► How do I get to ___?
Mai(n) ___ kaisé pahŭchŭ? मैं __ कैसे पहुँचूँ?
(Main ___ kai-say pa-hun-choon?)

► Can I walk there?
Kyā main vahān paidal jā saktā hŭ?
क्या मैं वहाँ पैदल जा सकता हूँ? (m. spkr)
(Kyaa main va-haan paidal jaa suk-taa hoon?)

Kyā main vahān paidal jā saktī hŭ?
क्या मैं वहाँ पैदल जा सकती हूँ? (f. spkr)
(Kyaa main va-haan paidal jaa suk-tee hoon?)

► What is the best way to get to ___?
**___ jāné ké liye sabsé achChhā sādhan kaun sā
hai?** ___ जाने का सबसे अच्छा साधन कौनसा है?
*(___ jaa-nay kaa sub-say ach-Chh-aa saa-dhan
kawn saa hai?)*

► Is it far?
Kyā vo bahut dūr hai? क्या वह बहुत दूर है?
(Kyaa vo bahut door hai?)

► Can you show me on the map?
Kyā āp nakshé mei(n) mujhé dikhā sakté hai(n)?
क्या आप नक्शे में मुझे दिखा सकते हैं?
*(Kyaa aap nuck-shay mein mujh-ay dikh-aa suk-
tay hain?)*

PART FOUR

Emergencies and Essentials; Lodging

AT THE POLICE STATION

complaint **shikāyat** शिकायत
(shi-kaa-yat)

offense **F.I.R.** एफ. आई. आर

thief **chōr** चोर
(cho-re)

theft **chorī** चोरी
(cho-ree)

An F.I.R. (First Information Report) is the initial written document that's prepared by the police.

▶ I want to file a complaint.
Mai(n) ék shikāyat darz karvānā chāhtā / chāhtī hū̃. मैं एक शिकायत दर्ज़ करवाना चाहता / चाहती हूँ|
(Mein ayk shi-kaa-yat der-z ker-vaa-naa chaah-taa/tee hoon.)

▶ I have to report an offense.
Mujhé F.I.R likhvānī hai. मुझे एफ.आई. आर लिखवानी है|
(Mujh-ay F.I.R likh-vaa-nee hai.)

► Someone has stolen my bag.
Kisi né mérā bag churā liyā hai.
किसी ने मेरा बैग चुरा लिया है|
(Ki-see-nay may-raa bag chu-raa li-yaa hai.)

► My passport has been stolen.
Méra passport chorī ho gayā hai.
मेरा पासपोर्ट चोरी हो गया है|
(May-raa paas-port cho-ree ho ga-yaa hai.)

► I have lost my ___.
Mérā ___ khō gayā hai. मेरा __ खो गया है|
(May-raa ___kho ga-yaa hai.)

► I have been raped.
Kisī né merī izzat lūT li hai. किसी ने मेरी इज़्ज़त लूट ली है|
(Ki-see nay may-ree iz-zat looT lee hai.)

► Someone is following me.
Koī mérā pīChhā kar rahā hai.
कोई मेरा पीछा कर रहा है|
(Ko-ee may-raa pee-Chhaa kar rhaa hai.)

► Someone has assaulted me.
Mujh par kisī né hamlā kiyā hai.
मुझ पर किसी ने हमला किया है|
(Mujh per kisee nay hum-laa ki-yaa hai.)

MEDICAL EMERGENCIES

sick/ill
bīmār बीमार
(bee-maar)

I am sick/ill.
Mai(n) bīmār hŭ. मैं बीमार हूँ।
(Main bee-maar hoon.)

hurts
dard
(der-d)

It hurts here.
Yahān dard hō rahā hai.
यहाँ दर्द हो रहा है।
(Ya-haan de-rd ho ra-haa hai.)

dizziness
chakkar
(chuk-ker)

I am feeling dizzy.
Mujhé chakkar ā rahé hai(n).
मुझे चक्कर आ रहे हैं।
(Mujh-ay chuk-ker aa ra-hey hain.)

headache
sir dard
(sir der-d)

I have a headache.
Méré sir mei(n) dard hō rahā hai.
मेरे सिर में दर्द हो रहा है।
(May-ray sir mein der-d ho ra-haa hai.)

toothache
dānt mein dard
*(daant mein
der-d)*

I am having tooth ache.
Méré dāt mein dard hō rahā hai.
मेरे दाँत में दर्द हो रहा है।
(Mere daant main der-d ho ra-haa hai.)

fever
bukhār
(bu-khaar)

I have a high fever.
Mujhé táze bukhār hō rahā hai.
मुझे तेज़ बुखार हो रहा है।
(Mujh-ay tay-z bukh-aar ho raha hai.)

food poisoning	I've got food poisoning.
	Mujhé food poisoning hō gayī hai.
	मुझे फ़ूड पॉइज़निग हो गई है|
	(Mujh-ay food poi-son-ing ho ga-yee hai.)
	I have eaten some bad food.
	Mainé koi khrāb khānā khā liyā.
	मैंने कोई खराब खाना खा लिया है|
	(Main-nay ko-yee kh-raab khaa-naa khaa li-yaa hai.)
heat stroke	I've got heat stroke.
lū	**Mujhé lū lag gayī hai.**
(loo)	मुझे लू लग गयी है|
	(Mujh-ay loo lug ga-yee hai.)
heart attack	I am having a heart attack.
dil kā daurā	**Mujhé dil kā daurā parD rahā hai.**
(dil kaa dau-raa)	मुझे दिल का दौरा पड़ रहा है|
	(Mujh-ay dil kaa daw-raa pa-rD ra-haa hai.)
breathing problem	I can't breathe.
dam / sãs Phoolnā	**Mérī sãs phool rahi hai. /**
	Mérā dum phool raha hai.
(dum/saans phool-naa)	मेरी साँस फूल रही है /
	मेरा दम फूल रहा है|
	(May-ree saans phool rah-hee hai./ May-ree dum phool rah-haa hai.)

cut
cut jānā
(cut jaa-naa)

I have cut my hand.
Mérā hāth cut gayā hai.
मेरा हाथ कट गया है|
(May-ra haa-th cut ga-yaa hai.)

injury
chot
(cho-T)

I am injured.
Mujhé chōt lag gayī hai.
मुझे चोट लग गई है|
(Mujh-ay cho-T lag ga-yee hai.)

blood
khun
(kh-oon)

I am bleeding.
Méré khūn nikal rahā hai.
मेरे खून निकल रहा है|
(May-ray kh-oon ni-kul ra-haa hai.)

wound
ghāv
(gh-aav)

My wound is bleeding.
Méré ghāv sé khūn nikal rahā hai.
मेरे घाव से खून निकल रहा है|
(May-ray gh-aav say kh-oon ni-kul ra-haa hai.)

▶ Please call an ambulance quickly.
Jaldī sé ambulance bulāo. जल्दी से एम्बूलेंस बुलाओ|
(Jul-dee say ambu-lance bu-laao.)

fire
āg
(aag)

Fire! Fire! (Shout in case of fire)
(Aag! Aag!) आग! आग!
(Aag! Aag!)

ACCOMMODATIONS

Most Indian cities, whether they're big or small, provide a huge selection of hotels for any budget. You can also find state-run tourist bungalows in every state; this is an affordable option. If you want to experience the India lifestyle "up close and personal," consider staying with a family who provides services in alliance with Tourism Development Corporations, for example those of Rajasthan, Laddakh, Chennai and Mumbai.

room	**kamrā** कमरा *(kum-raa)*
rooms	**kamré** कमरे *(kum-ray)*
room charge	**kamré kā chārge** कमरे का चार्ज *(kum-ray kaa chaar-ge)*
room key	**kamré kī chābī** कमरे की चाबी *(kum-ray kee chaa-bee)*
facilities	**suvidhāé** सुविधाएँ *(su-vi-dhaa-yen)*
bedding	**bistar** बिस्तर *(bis-ter)*
comforter	**razāyī** रज़ाई *(razaa-ee)*
pillow	**takiyā** तकिया *(tuck-ee-yaa)*
sheet	**chādar** चादर *(chaa-der)*
mattress	**gaddā** गद्दा *(gad-daa)*

single bed	**ék bistar wālā** एक बिस्तर वाला
	(ayk bis-ter waa-laa)
double bed	**do bistrò wālā** दो बिस्तरों वाला
	(tho bis-teron waa-laa)
bath	**gusal khānā** गुसलखाना
	(guh-sul-khaa-naa)

MAKING RESERVATIONS

▶ Do you have a room available?
Kyā āpké pās ék kamrā milégā?
क्या आपके पास एक कमरा मिलेगा।
(Kyaa aap-kay paas ayk kum-raa mil-ay-gaa.)

▶ I want to book a room.
Main ék kamrā book karānā chāhtā hů̃. (m. spkr)
मैं एक कमरा बुक कराना चाहता हूँ।
(Main ayk kum-raa book ker-aa-naa chaa-h-taa hoon.)

Main ék kamrā book karānā chāhtī hů̃. (f. spkr)
मैं एक कमरा बुक कराना चाहती हूँ।
(Main ayk kum-raa book ker-aa-naa chaa-h-tee hoon.)

Hum ék kamrā book karānā chāhté hain. (pl.)
हम एक कमरा बुक कराना चाहते हैं।
(Hum ayk kum-raa book ker-aa-naa chaa-h-tay hain.)

► We need two rooms with double beds.
Hamé double bed wālé do kamré chāhiyé.
हमें डबल बैड वाले दो कमरे चाहिए।
(Hum-ein double bed waa-lay tho kum-ray chaa-hi-yayn.)

BANKING AND MONEY

Indian paper currency is called **rupiya** (rupee). The **paisa** is equal to 1/100th of a rupee. You'll notice that the word "**paisa**" is also often used as a synonym for money or cash. Indian rupee notes come in Rs.5, Rs.10, Rs.20, Rs.50, Rs.100, Rs.500 and Rs.1000. One- and two-rupee notes have been discontinued in the paper form, but are still in circulation as coins. Coins in India are available in seven denominations: 10 paise, 20 paise, 25 paise, 50 paise, one rupee, two rupees and five rupees.

currency	**mudrā** मुद्रा *(mud-raa)*	
exchange rate	**exchange rate** ऐक्सचेंज रेट *(ex-change ray-t)*	
U.S. dollars	**amrīkī dollar** अमरीकी डॉलर *(am-ree-kee doll-ar)*	
traveler's check	**traveler's check** ट्रैवलर्स चैक *(traveler's check)*	

► What is the current exchange rate?
Abhi kī exchange rate kyā hai?
अभी की ऐक्सचेंज रेट क्या है?
(Abh-ee kee exchange rate kyaa hai?)

▶ Where can I exchange dollars?
Main dollars kahān badalwā saktā hū̃?
मैं डॉलर्स कहाँ बदलवा सकता हूँ?
(Main dollars ka-haan ba-dull-waa suk-taa hoon)

▶ Do you accept traveler's checks?
Kyā āp traveler's check léte hain?
क्या आप ट्रैवलर्स चैक लेते हैं?
(Kyaa aap traveler's check lay-tay hain?)

▶ Please give me small change for this.
Kripayā mujhé iské khullé dé dījiyé.
कृपया मुझे इसके खुल्ले दे दीजिए।
(kri-payaa mujh-a is-kay khul-lay day dee-ji-yay.)

▶ What time does the bank open?
Bank kitné bajé khultā hai?
बैंक कितने बजे खुलता है?
(Bank kit-nay baj-ay khul-taa hai?)

▶ I have no money with me.
Méré pās koi paisā nahīṅ hai.
मेरे पास कोई पैसा नहीं है।
(May-ray paas koi pai-saa na-heen hai.)

PART FIVE

In a Restaurant; Out and About

ORDERING FOOD AND PAYING THE BILL

breakfast	**nāshtā** नाश्ता
	(naa-sh-taa)
fruits	**phal** फल
	(pha-ul)
egg	**āDā** अंडा
	(un-Daa)
boiled egg	**ublā āDā** उबला अंडा
	(ub-laa un-Daa)
bread	**double roṭī** डबल रोटी
	(dub-ul ro-tee)
butter	**makkhan** मक्खन
	(muck-kh-un)
omelette	**āmlate** आमलेट
	(aam-late)
milk	**dūdh** दूध
	(doodh)
juice	**phalon kā ras** फलों का रस
	(phalon-kaa rus)
cold	**Thhandā** ठंडा
	(Thhun-daa)
hot	**garam** गरम
	(ger-um)

tea	**chāi** चाय *(chaay)*
sugar	**chīnī** चीनी *(chee-nee)*
spicy	**masalédār** मसालेदार *(mus-aa-lay-daar)*
lunch	**din kā khānā** दिन का खाना *(din kaa khaa-naa)*
bread	**rotī / chapātī** रोटी / चपाती *(ro-tee / chup-aa-tee)*
rice	**chāval** चावल *(chaa-vul)*
vegetable	**sabzī** सब्ज़ी *(sub-zee)*
lentil	**dāl** दाल *(daal)*
yogurt	**dahī** दही *(duhee)*
pickle	**achār** अचार *(uch-r)*
yogurt relish	**raitā** रायता *(raay-taa)*
potato pastry	**samosā** समोसा *(sumo-saa)*
chutney (relish)	**chutnī** चटनी *(chut-nee)*
fritters	**pakodā** पकोड़ा *(puck-orDaa)*
sherbet	**sherbet** शरबत *(sher-but)*

water	**pānī** पानी *(paa-nee)*
ice	**baraf** बरफ़ *(bur-uff)*
dinner	**rāt kā khānā** रात का खाना *(raat kaa khaa-naa)*
vegetarian	**shākāhārī** शाकाहरी *(shaa-kaa haa-ree)*
non-vegetarian	**māsāhārī** माँसाहारी *(maansaa-haa-ree)*
chicken	**murgī** मुर्गी *(mur-gee)*
roasted	**bhunā** भुना *(bhu-naa)*
meat	**gosht** गोश्त *(go-sht)*
goat	**bakrā** बकरा *(buck-raa)*
nan (flat bread)	**nān** नान *(naan)*
fish	**muChlī** मछ्ली *(muChh-lee)*
sweets	**mithaī** मिठाई *(mi-Thhaa-yee)*
menu	**mīnū** मीनू *(mee-noo)*

When you go to a restaurant in India, remember not to ask for beef or pork. A majority of the population in India is either Hindu or Muslim; the cow is considered by Hindus to be sacred, and pork is considered unhygienic by Muslims.

▶ Excuse me!
   Suniyé! सुनिए!
   (Suni-yay!)

▶ What do you have for breakfast?
   Āpké pās nāshté mein kyā-kyā hai?
   आपके पास नाश्ते में क्या-क्या है?
   (Aap-kay paas naa-sh-tay mein kyaa-kyaa hai?)

▶ What do you have for lunch?
   Āpké pās din ké khāné mein kyā-kyā hai?
   आपके पास दिन के खाने में क्या-क्या है?
   (Aap-kay paas din kay khaa-nay mein kyaa-kyaa hai?)

▶ I would like an omelette, butter and toast and a cup of coffee.
   Mujhé ék āmlate, makkhan, toast aur ék cup coffee chāhiyé.
   मुझे एक आमलेट, मक्खन, टोस्ट और एक कप कॉफ़ी चाहिए|
   (Mujh-ay ayk aam-late muck-khun, TowsT, aur ayk cup coffee chaa-hi-yay.)

▶ Do you have any bottled water?
   Kyā āpké pās pāni kī botal hai?
   क्या आपके पास पानी की बोतल है?
   (Kyaa aap-kay paas paa-nee kee bo-tul hai?)

▶ Do you have a menu in English?
   Kyā āpké pās English mei(n) mīnū hai?
   क्या आपके पास इंगलिश में मीनू है?
   (Kyaa aap-kay paas English mein mee-noo hai?)

▶ Can you make less spicy food?
   Kyā āp kam tīkhā khānā banā sakté hain?
   क्या आप कम तीखा खाना बना सकते हैं?
   (Kyaa aap kum tee-khaa khaa-naa bun-aa suk tay hain?)

▶ Please get me my bill.
   Bill lay āiyé. बिल ले आइये|
   (Bill lay aa-iyay.)

▶ Do you take credit cards?
   Kyā āp credit cārd léte hai(n)?
   क्या आप क्रैडिट कार्ड लेते हैं?
   (Kyaa-aap credit card lay-tay hain?)

SHOPPING

India is a shopping paradise for foreign travelers and shop-aholics alike. On one hand, its bazaars are bustling with multistoried shopping malls and high-class boutiques for those who have lots to spend; on the other hand, the true color of the Indian bazaars can be seen through its local artisans and midsized businesspeople who offer a variety of goods at reasonable prices to fit anyone's budget.

market	**bāzār** बाज़ार
	(baa-zaar)
shop	**dukān** दुकान
	(du-kaan)
shop keeper	**dukāndār** दुकानदार
	(du-kaan-daar)

price	**bhāv / kīmat / dām** भाव / क़ीमत / दाम
	(bhaav / qee-mut / daam)
receipt	**rasīd** रसीद
	(rus-eed)
balance	**bakāyā** बक़ाया
	(buck-aa-yaa)
refund	**paise lauTānā** पैसे लौटाना
	(pai-say law-Taa-naa)
remaining money	**bākī paisé** बाक़ी पैसे
	(baaqee pai-say)
cloth store	**kaprDé kī dukān** कपड़े की दुकान
	(kup-rDay ki du-kaan)
shoe store	**juté ki dukān** जूते की दुकान
	(joo-tay kee du-kaan)
cobbler	**mochī** मोची
	(mow-chi)
cash	**nakad** नक़द
	(nuqad)
credit	**udhār** उधार
	(udhaar)
credit card	**credit card** क्रैडिट कार्ड
	(credit card)
special	**vishésh / khās** विशेष / ख़ास
	(vish-a-sh / khaas)
discount	**ChhūT** छूट
	(ChhooT)
expensive	**mahangā** (m.) **/ mahngī** (f.) **/ mehngé** (pl.) महँगा / महँगी / महँगे
	(meh-gaa / meh-gee / meh-gay)
cheap	**sastā / sastī / sasté** सस्ता / सस्ती / सस्ते
	(sus-taa / sus-tee / sus-tay)

of good quality	**barDhiyā quality kā** बढ़िया क्वालिटी का *(burD-iyaa quality kaa)*
bargaining	**mol-bhāv** मोलभाव *(mole-bhaav)*
pharmacy	**dawāī kī dukān** दवाई की दुकान *(duwaa-ee kee du-kaan)*

PURCHASING & BARGAINING

Bargaining is a big part of the Indian mindset. Most of the vendors and shop keepers maintain a certain margin for the bargaining, and if you bargain with them, they sometimes do reduce the amount substantially. Stores such as pharmacies, book stores, stationery or greeting card shops, gift shops, and showrooms usually do not bargain—they generally keep to a fixed price.

▶ How much is it?
Yeh kitné kā hai? यह कितने का है?
(Yeh kit-nay kaa hai?)

▶ How much are they?
Yeh kitné ké diyé? यह कितने के दिए?
(Yeh kit-nay kay di-yay?)

▶ What is its price?
Iskā dām kyā hai? इसका दाम क्या है?
(Is-kaa daam kyaa hai?)

► What is the price for this item?
Isé kis bhāv mein dé rahé hain?
इसे किस भाव में दे रहे हैं?
(Is-ay kis bhaav mein day rah-ay hain?)

► Show me a good quality one.
Mujhé barDhiyā quality kā dikhāiyé.
मुझे बढ़िया क्वालिटी का दिखाइये|
(Mujh-ay berDhiyaa quality kaa dikhaa-iyay)

► Where can I find this?
Yeh kahằ milégā? यह कहाँ मिलेगा?
(Yeh ka-ha(n) mil-ay-gaa?)

► Do you take credit cards?
Kyā āp credit card lété hain?
क्या आप क्रैडिट कार्ड लेते हैं?
(Kyaa-aap credit card lay-tay hain?)

► Do you have change for five hundred rupees?
Kyā āpké pās pằch sau ké khulé hồgé / milégé?
क्या आपके पास पाँच सौ रुपये के खुल्ले होंगे / मिलेंगे?
(Kyaa aap-kay paas paanch saw rupay kay khullay ho-ng-ay / mil-a-ng-ay?)

► Can you tell me where can I find this?
Kyā āp mujhé batā sakté hain ki yeh kahằ milégā?
क्या आप मुझे बता सकते हैं कि यह कहाँ मिलेगा?
(Kyaa aap mujh-ay but-aa suk-tay hain ki yeh ka-haàn mil-ay-gaa?)

► Please reduce the price.
thorDā kam kījīyé. थोड़ा कम कीजिए|
(thorDaa kum kee-ji-yay.)

► Give me the right price.
Thhīk Thhīk boliyé. ठीक-ठीक बोलिए|
(Thheek-Thheek bow-lee-yay.)

► That's too high, give me a better price.
**Āp bahut zyādā bol rahé hain. Thīk lagāiye /
lagāo.**
आप बहुत ज़्यादा बोल रहे हैं | ठीक लगाइये / लगाओ|
*(Aap bahut zyaa-daa bol rah-a hain, Thheek lag-
aa-iyay / lag-aa-o.)*

► Can you show me one at a lower price than this?
Mujhé is sé kam dām kā dikhāiyé?
मुझे इस से कम दाम का दिखाइये?
(Mujh-ay is say kum daam kaa dikh-aa-ee-yay?)

► Can you ship these things to ___?
Kyā āp yé sāmān ___ bhijvā sakté hai(n)?
क्या आप ये सामान ___ भिजवा सकते हैं?
*(Kyaa aap yay saa-maan ___ bhij-waa suktay
hain?)*

► I need to return this item.
Mujhé yé sāmān vāpas lauTānā hai.
मुझे यह सामान वापस लौटाना है|
(Mujh-ay yay saa-maan vaa-pus law-Taa-naa hai.)

AT A BOOK STORE

book	**kitāb** किताब *(ki-taab)*
novel	**upanyās** उपन्यास *(oop-un-nyaas)*
magazine	**patrikā** पत्रिका *(putt-rickaa)*
newspaper	**akhbār** अख़बार *(uckh-bar)*
map	**nakshā** नक़्शा *(nuq-shaa)*
religious	**dhārmick** धार्मिक *(dhaar-mick)*
political	**rājnītik** राजनीतिक *(raaj-nee-tik)*
music	**sangīt** संगीत *(sung-eet)*
children's books	**bachchò ki kitabé** बच्चों की किताबें *(buchch-on kee ki-taa-ben)*
playing cards	**tāsh** ताश *(taa-sh)*
chess	**shatranj** शतरंज *(shut-runj)*
dictionary	**shabdkosh** शब्दकोश *(shubd-kosh)*

▶ Do you have a map of Delhi?
Kyā āpké pās Dillī kā nakshā hai?
क्या आपके पास दिल्ली का नक़्शा है?
(Kyaa aap-kay paas dilli kaa nuq-shaa hai?)

▶ Do you also carry children's board games?
Kyā āp bachchó ké board games bhī rakhté hain?
क्या आप बच्चों के बोर्ड गेम्स भी रखते हैं?
(Kyaa aap buch-cho kay board games bhee ruckh-tay hain?)

▶ I need an English-to-Hindi dictionary.
Mujhe English se Hindi kā ék shabdkosh / ki dictionary chahiye. मुझे इंगलिश से हिन्दी का एक शब्दकोश | की डिक्शनरी चाहिए|
(Mujh-ay ayk English say Hindi kaa shubd-kosh / key dictionary chaa-hi-yay.)

▶ Plaese give me today's English newspaper.
Mujhé āj kā English kā akhbār dé dījiyé.
मुझे आज का इंगलिश का अख़बार दे दीजिए|
(Mujh-ay aaj kaa English kaa uckh-baar day dee-ji-yay.)

▶ May I sit here and read?
Kyā mai(n) yahǎ baiThhkar parDh saktā hǔ?
क्या मैं यहाँ बैठकर पढ़ सकता हूँ?
(Kyaa main ya-haan baiThh-kerr parDh suk-taa hoon?)

AT A CLOTHING STORE

saree	**sārDī** साड़ी *(saa-rDee)*
blouse	**blouze** ब्लाउज़ *(bla-uze)*
petticoat	**petticoat** पेटीकोट *(pay-tea-coat)* (The main undergarment worn with a saree; it's usually ankle length.)
tunic	**kurtā** कुर्ता *(kur-taa)*
loose pants for women	**salwār** सलवार *(sul-waar)*
pajama	**pajāmā** पजामा *(puj-aa-maa)*
shirt	**kamīz** क़मीज़ *(kum-eez)*
silk	**résham** रेशम *(ray-shum)*
silken	**réshmi** रेशमी *(ray-shmee)*
hand spun cotton	**khādī** खादी *(khaa-dee)*
skirt (modern)	**skirt** स्कर्ट *(skirt)*
skirt (traditional)	**léhngā** लहँगा *(leh-ngaa)*
girl's dress	**frock** फ़्रॉक *(frock)*
handkerchief	**rumāl** रुमाल *(ru-maal)*

underwear	**chaDDī** चड्डी
	(chuD-Dee)
undershirt	**baniyān** बनियान
	(buni-yaan)
long coat	**achkan / shérwānī**
(for males)	अचकन / शेरवानी
	(uch-kun / sheyr-waa-nee)
socks	**mozé** मोज़े
	(mow-zay)
hat	**topī** टोपी
	(tow-pee)

▶ What is this shirt made out of?
Yeh kamīz kis kaprDé se banī hai?
यह क़मीज़ किस कपड़े से बनी है?
(Yeh qameez kis kuprDay say buni hai?)

▶ May I see some good silk sarees? [i.e., Please show
us some good silk sarees.]
Humė kuch achChī reshmī sārDiyā̃ dikhāiyé.
हमें कुछ अच्छी रेशमी साड़ियाँ दिखाइये|
*(Hum-ain kuChh uch-Chhee ray-shmee saarD-
iyaan dikhaa-iyay.)*

▶ I want to buy few cotton kurtas.
Main kuCh sutī kurté kharīdnā chāhtā hũ.
मैं कुछ सूती कुर्ते खरीदना चाहता हूँ|
*(Main kuChh soo-tee kur-tay kher-eednaa chaah-
taa hoon.)*

MEASUREMENTS & SIZES

measurement
nāp नाप
(naap)

weight
bhār / tol भार / तोल
(bhaar / tole)

length
lambāi लंबाई
(lumb-aa-ee)

width
chaurDāi चौड़ाई
(chaw-rDaa-ee)

height
ūnchāī ऊँचाई
(oon-chaa-ee)

breadth
arz अर्ज़
(urz)

kilogram
kilo किलो
(kilo)

half a kilo
ādhā kilo आधा किलो
(aadhaa-kilo)

250 grams
pāv पाव
(paav)

yard
gaz गज़
(guz)

▶ Please measure it properly.
Isé Thhīk sé nāpiyé / nāpo. इसे ठीक से नापिए / नापो|
(Isay Thheek say naap-iyay / naa-po.)

▶ Please weigh it properly
Isé Thhīk sé toliyé / tolo. इसे ठीक से तोलिए / तोलो|
(Isay Theek say tow-liyay / tow-lo.)

▶ Give me 250 grams of ____.
  Mujhé pāvbhar ___ dénā. मुझे पाव-भर __ देना|
  (Mujh-ay paav-bhur ___ day-naa.)

In this book we have provided two ways of requesting things in a market while shopping in India. For instance, the polite form of the verb "to give" is **dījīyé** or **dé dījīye** *(dee-ji-yay / day-dee-ji-yay)* which can be used at shops such as clothes, shoe, and book stores, post offices, or any other high-end shops, whereas the neutral form of verb "to give," **dénā** *(day-naa)*, is most often used with vegetable vendors, fruit sellers, roadside small vendors, makeshift stores and hawkers. The village folk or lower end of the Indian society generally do not use the polite forms of verbs while speaking or dealing with others.

AT THE POST OFFICE

mail	**dāk** डाक *(daak)*
letter	**patra / chiTThhī** चिट्ठी *(putruh / chit-Thee)*
post office	**dāk ghar** डाकघर *(daak-ghar)*
main post office	**mukhya dāk ghar** मुख्य डाकघर *(mukhy-daak-ghar)*
inland letter (within India)	**antardéshiya patra** अंतर्देशीय पत्र *(unter desh-iy-putt-ra)*
envelope	**lifāfā** लिफ़ाफ़ा *(lifaa-faa)*

stamp/postage	**dāk tickat** डाक टिकट
	(daak ti-cut)
airmail	**hawāi patra** हवाई पत्र
	(huwaa-ee putt-ra)
registered mail	**registry** रजिस्ट्री
	(regis-tree)
message	**sandésh** संदेश
	(sun-desh)
address	**patā** पता
	(putt-aa)
ZIP code	**pincode** पिन कोड
	(pin-code)
fax	**fax** फ़ैक्स
signature	**hastakshar / dastakhat**
	हस्ताक्षर / दस्तख़त
	(hust-aak-shur / dust-ukh-ut)

▶ I have to send this letter to___.
  Mujhé yeh patra ___ bhéjnā hai.
  मुझे यह पत्र...... भेजना है।
  (Mujh-ay yeh putt-ra___ bhayj-naa hai.)

▶ How much will it cost to send this letter to___?
  Yeh patra ___ bhejné mai(n) kitnā lagégā?
  यह पत्र __ भेजने में कितना लगेगा?
  (Yeh putt-ra ___ bhay-jnay mein kitnaa lugay gaa?)

▶ Three 3-rupee stamps please.
  Teen rupaiy ké tīn tickat dé dījiyé.
  तीन रुपये के तीन टिकट दे दीजिए।
  (Teen rupay kay teen ti-cut day dee-gji-yay.)

► I have to send this parcel outside of India.
  Mujhé yeh parcel bhārat sé bāhar bhijwānā hai.
  मुझे यह पार्सल भारत से बाहर भिजवाना है।
  (Mujh-ay yeh parcel bhaa-rut say baa-her bhij-waa-naa hai.)

► I have to have this registered.
  Mujhé iskī registry karwāni hai.
  मुझे इसकी रजिस्ट्री करवानी है।
  (Mujh-ay is-kee regis-tree ker-waa-nee hai.)

► My name is ___. I am expecting money from___.
  Has it arrived yet?
  Mérā nām ___ hai. ___ sé méré paisé ānewālé hai.
  Kyā méré paise āgayé hai(n)?
  (May-raa naam ___ hai. ___say may-ray pai-say
  aanay-waalay hain. Kyaa may-ray pai-say aa-
  guyay hain?)
  मेरा नाम ___ है।. ___ से मेरे पैसे आने वाले हैं। क्या मेरे पैसे
  आ गये हैं?

► Where do I have to sign?
  Mujhé hastākhsar kahȧ karné hai?
  मुझे हस्ताक्षर कहाँ करने हैं?
  (Mujh-a hust-aak-sher ka-haan kernay hain?)

AT A PHARMACY

medicine	**davā / davāī** दवा / दवाई
	(duwaa / duwaa-ee)
ayurvedic medicine	**aushadhī** औषधि
	(aw-shudhi)
pharmacy	**davākhānā** दवाखाना
	(duwaa-khaa-naa)
ayurvedic pharmacy	**āyurvedic aushdhālay**
	आयुर्वेदिक औषधालय
	(aa-yur-vedic awe-shdh-aaluy)
prescription	**parchī / nuskhā** पर्ची / नुस्ख़ा
	(per-chee / nus-khaa)
injection	**injection / sūī** इंजैक्शन / सूई
	(in-jack-shun / sue-ee)
vaccination	**Tīkā** टीका
	(Tee-kaa)
bandage	**pattī** पट्टी
	(putt-ee)
ointment	**malham** मलहम
	(mull-hum)
Dettol antiseptic liquid	**Dettol** डिटॉल
	(dit-all)

(Dettol is a brand of liquid antiseptic commonly found in India.)

▶ Please give me these medicines.
   Mujhé yeh dawāiyā̃ dé dījīyé.
   मुझे ये दवाइयाँ दे दीजिए|
   (Mujh-ay yeh duwaa-e-yaan day-dee-ji-yay.)

► I need a muscle relaxant.
  Mujhé ék muscle relaxant chāhiyé.
  मुझे एक मसल रिलैक्सैंट चाहिए|
  (Mujh-ay ayk muscle relaxant chaa-he-yay.)

► How much is a bottle of Dettol?
  Dettol kī botal kitné kī hai?
  डिटॉल की बोतल कितने की है?
  (Dit-all kee bo-tul kit-nay kee hai?)

► What time should I come back?
  Main kitné bajé vāpas aū̃?
  मैं कितने बजे वापस आऊँ?
  (Main kitnay buj-ay vaa-puss aa-oon?)

AT THE BARBERSHOP

A barbershop in India is meant for men and boys. If you are a female and need to have your hair done, look for a beauty parlor instead—they can be found everywhere in India, run only by women. Unisex salons can also be found in some high-end areas in cities such as Delhi or Bombay. Some barbers also set up their makeshift shops underneath a tree. They usually also offer head massages and some body massage (like shoulders, head, neck). Cheap yet enjoyable!

barber	**nāī** नाई
	(naa-ee)
hair	**bāl** बाल
	(baal)
beard	**dārDhī** दाढ़ी
	(daa-rDhee)
moustache	**mūch** मूँछ
	(moon-Chh)
shaving	**shaving** शेविंग
	(shay-wing)
head massage	**sir kī mālish** सिर की मालिश
	(sir kee maa-lish)
razor	**ustrā** उस्तरा
	(oos-traa)
massage	**mālish** मालिश
	(maa-lish)

▶ I need to have my hair cut.
   Mujhé bāl katwāné hain. मुझे बाल कटवाने हैं|
   (Mujh-ay baal cut-waa-nay hain.)

► I need to have my beard done.
Mujhé apnī dārDhī banvānī hai.
मुझे अपनी दाढ़ी बनवानी है।
(Mujh-ay up-nee daa-rDhee bun-waa-nee hai.)

► Could you please massage my head too?
Kyā méré sir kī mālish bhī kar dégé?
क्या मेरे सिर की मालिश कर देंगें?
(Kyaa may-ray sir kee maa-lish bhee kar day-ngay?)

► How much do I owe you?
Kitné hué / mujhé āpkō kitné déné hain?
कितने हुए / मुझे आपको कितने देने हैं?
(Kitnay huay / mujh-a aapko kitnay day-nay hain?)

► Keep the change.
Bākī ké paise rakh lo. बाक़ी के पैसे रख लो।
(Baa-qee kay paise ruckh lo.)

This you can say to a roadside barber, but not in a beauty parlor or a salon. There you'd instead give a tip. However, it is better to give some kind of tip to whomever provides you any type of service, the same way you would in your own country.

AT THE BEAUTY SALON

eyebrows	**bhòhé̃** भौंहें
	(bhon-hain)
threading	**threading** थ्रैडिंग
	(threading)
plucking	**plucking** प्लकिंग
	(plucking)
henna	**méhndī** मेंहदी
	(meh-ndee)
make-up	**shringār / make-up** श्रृंगार / मेकअप
	(shring-aar / make-up)
nails	**nākhūn** नाखून
	(naa-khoon)

▶ I need to have my hair set.
Mujhé apné bāl set karvāné hain.
मुझे अपने बाल सैट करवाने हैं|
(Mujh-ay up-nay baal set kerwaa-nay hain.)

▶ I want to have henna on my hands.
Main apné hathõ par méhndī lagvānā chāhtī hū̃.
मैं अपने हाथों पर मेंहदी लगवाना चाहती हूँ|
(Main up-nay haa-thon per mehn-dee lag-waa-naa chaah-tee hoon.)

▶ I want to have my hair colored.
Main apné bāl rangvānā chāhtī hū̃.
मैं अपने बाल रंगवाना चाहती हूँ|
(Main up-nay baal rung-waa-naa chaah-tee hoon.)

► Can you cut my hair in this style?
  Kyā āp méré bāl is tarah kāt sakté hain?
  क्या आप मेरे बाल इस तरह काट सकते हैं?
  (Kyaa aap may-ray baal iss ter-ha kaat suk-tay hain?)

USING THE TELEPHONE / CELL PHONES

telephone	**dūrbhāsh / phone** दूरभाष / फोन *(door-bhaa-sh / phone)*
P.C.O	**P.C.O** पी.सी.ओ In a Public Call Office, you pay the shop owner for use of the public phone.
cell phone	**mobile** मोबाइल
rate	**dar** दर *(der)*
per minute	**pratī minut** प्रति मिनट *(pruti minut)*
STD	**Standard Trunk Dialing**
ISD	**International Trunk Dialing**
Pre-paid card	**charge card**

► Can I make an international call from here?
  Kyā main yahā̃ sé ék international call kar saktā hū̃? क्या मैं यहाँ से एक इंटरनैशनल कॉल कर सकता हूँ?
  (Kyaa main ya-haan say ayk international call ker suk-taa hoon?)

▶ Where can I make a local call?

Main yahã local call kahã sé kar sakta hũ?

मैं यहाँ लोकल कॉल कहाँ से कर सकता हूँ?

(Main ya-haan local call ka-haan say ker suk-taa hoon?)

▶ What is the rate to make a phone call to ___?

___ phone karné kī dar / rate kyā hai?

__ फ़ोन करने की दर / रेट क्या है?

(___ phone ker-nay kee der / rate kyaa hai?)

▶ Do you know the code for ___? (country / state / city)

Kyā āpko ___ (desh / rajya / shahar) kā code mālum hai?

क्या आपको __ (देश / राज्य / शहर) का कोड मालूम है?

(Kyaa aap-ko ___ (deish / raj-ya / sha-har) kaa code maa-loom hai?)

▶ Do you sell SIM cards for cell phones?

Kyā āp mobile phone kā sim card béchté hain?

क्या आप मोबाइल फ़ोन का सिम कार्ड बेचते हैं?

(Kyaa aap mobile phone kaa sim card bay-ch-tay hain?)

▶ Can I get a pre-paid phone card?

Mujhé ék charge card chāhiyé. Āpké pās hai?

मुझे एक चार्ज कार्ड चाहिए| क्या आपके पास है?

(Mujh-ay ayk charge card chaa-he-yay. Aap-kay paas hai?)

PART SIX

Enjoying India

▶ Are you ready?
Kyā āp taiyār hain? क्या आप तैयार हैं?
(Kyaa aap tay-yaar hain?)

▶ Shall we go?
Chalain? चलें?
(chal-ain?)

▶ Let's go!
Chalo chalé! चलो, चलें!
(chal-ow chal-ain!)

HOLIDAYS

When you visit India, you'll likely have the chance to learn about a holiday—many holidays and celebrations take place all year round. It's a time to see the many colors of India, to taste the diverse culture, to dance, and to live!

New Year   **Nayā sāl / Nav versh**
नया साल / नव वर्ष
(Na-yaa saal / Nuv versh)

Mid Winter   **LohrDī** लोहड़ी
  Harvest Festival   *(Lowh-rDee)*
  (Jan. 13, Punjab
  and North India)

Mid Winter Harvest Festival (Jan. 15, Tamilnadu)	**Pongal** पोंगल *(Pong-ul)*
Republic Day (Jan. 26)	**GarNtantra Diwas** गणतंत्र दिवस *(GerN-tuntr-diw-us)*
Neta ji's birthday (Jan. 23)	**Nétājī Diwas** नेता जी दिवस *(Nay-taa-g diwus)*
Festival of Colors (March–April)	**Holī** होली *(Ho-lee)*
Prophet Muhammad's Birthday (February)	**Milad-ul-Nabi** मिलाद-उल-नबी *(Mi-laad-ul-nub-ee)*
Lord Ram's Birthday (April)	**Rām navamī** राम नवमी *(Raam nuv-mee)*
Good Friday (April)	**Good Friday** गुड फ़्राइडे *(Good Friday)*
Easter (April)	**Easter** ईस्टर *(Easter)*
Harvest Festival (April 13, Punjab)	**Baisākhī** बैसाखी *(Bai-saa-khee)*
Harvest Festival (April 15, Assam's New Year)	**Rongāli Bīhu** रोंगाली बीहू *(Rongaa-lee bee-hoo)*
May Day / Labor Day (May 1)	**Shramik diwas** श्रमिक दिवस *(Shrum-ick diwus)*
Lord Buddha's Birthday (May full Moon)	**Budh Pūrnimā** बुद्ध पूर्णिमा *(Buddh poorn-imaa)*
Full moon day to observe Gurus (July full Moon)	**Guru Pūrnimā** गुरु पूर्णिमा *(Guru poorn-imaa)*

Goddess Parvati's Communion with Lord Shiva (Aug., Rajasthan, Haryana & Punjab)	**teej** तीज *(teej)*
Lord Ganesha's Birthday (September)	**Ganesh chaturthī** गणेश चतुर्थी *(Gun-eish chut-ur-thee)*
Independence Day (August 15)	**Swatantrtā diwas** स्वतंत्रता दिवस *(Swut-untr-taa diwus)*
Festival for brothers and sisters (August full moon)	**Rakshā Bandhan** रक्षा बंधन *(Ruck-shaa bun-dhun)*
Lord Krishna's Birthday (Aug./Sept.)	**Janmāshtmī** जन्माष्टमी *(Jun-maash-Tmee)*
End of Ramadan (August)	**Īd-ul-fitr** ईद-उल-फ़ितर *(Eed-ul fitr)*
Harvest Festival (Aug./Sept., Kerela)	**Onam** ओणम *(O-rNum)*
Teacher's Day (Sept. 5)	**Shikshak Diwas** शिक्षक दिवस *(Shick-shuck diwus)*
Worshipping Goddess Durga (September / October)	**Durgā Pujā** दुर्गा पूजा *(Dur-gaa poo-jaa)*
Nine-day celebration (October)	**Navrātrī** नवरात्रि *(Nuv-raat-ri)*
Mahatma Gandhi's Birthday (Oct. 2)	**Gāndhī jayantī** गाँधी जयंती *(Gaan-dhee Juy-untee)*
Fasting by married women (October)	**Karvā Chauth** करवा चौथ *(Ker-waa chau-th)*

Lord Ram's Victory Day (~October)	**Dusséhrā** दशहरा *(duss-eh-raa)*
Worshipping the protector of wealth (~November)	**Dhantéras** धनतेरस *(dhun-tey-rus)*
Festival of Lights (New moon night between mid-October and mid-November)	**Deepāwalī / Diwālī** दीपावली / दिवाली *(deep-aa-wulee / di-waa-lee)*
Pushkar Cattle Fair (5 days, November–December)	**Pushkar Pashū Mélā** पुष्कर पशु मेला *(Push-ker Pashu May-laa)*
Children's Day (Nov. 14, Nehru's Birthday)	**Bāl Diwas** बाल दिवस *(Baal diwus)*
Christmas (Dec. 25)	**BarDā Din** बड़ा दिन *(BerDaa din)*

HOLIDAY GREETINGS

▶ Happy New Year!
Nav varsh kī shubhkāmnāyé! / Nayā sal mubāraq ho! नव वर्ष की शुभकामनाएँ! / नया साल मुबारक़ हो!
(Nuv ver-sh kee shubh-kaam-naayen! / Nuyaa saal mubaa-ruq ho!)

▶ Happy Republic Day!
GarNtantra diwas ki shubhkāmnāyé! / GarNtantra diwas kī badhāyī! गणतंत्र दिवस की शुभकामनाएँ! / गणतंत्र दिवस की बधाई!
(GurN-tuntr diwus kee shubh-kaam-naayen! / GurN-tantr diwus kee budhaa-yee!)

► Happy Independence Day!

Swatantrtā diwas kī shubhkāmnāyè! / diwas kī badhāyī! स्वतंत्रता दिवस की शुभकामनाएँ / स्वतंत्रता दिवस की बधाई!

(Swa-tun-trtaa diwus kee shubh-kaam-naayen / Swa-tun-trtaa diwus kee budhaa-yee!)

► Happy Holi!

Holī kī rām-rām! / Holī kī hārdik shubhkāmnāyè! / Holī mubāraq! होली की राम-राम! / होली की हार्दिक शुभकामानाएँ! / होली मुबारक़!

(Ho-lee kee raam-raam! / Ho-lee kee haar-dik shubh-kaam-naayen! / Ho-lee mubaa-ruq!)

► Happy Diwali!

Diwālī kī rām-rām! / Diwālī kī hārdik shubhkāmnāyè! / Diwālī mubāraq! दिवाली की राम-राम! / दिवाली की हार्दिक शुभकामानाएँ! / दिवाली मुबारक़!

(diwaa-lee kee raam-raam! / diwaa-lee kee haar-dik shubh-kaam-naayen! / diwaa-lee mubaa-ruq!)

► Happy Id!

Īd Mubāraq! ईद मुबारक़!

(Eed Mubaa-ruq!)

► Happy birthday!

Janam din kī badhāī! / Janam din mubāraq ho! / Sālgirah mubāraq ho! जन्मदिन की बधाई! / जन्मदिन मुबारक़ हो! / सालगिरह मुबारक़ हो!

(Junum din kee budhaa-yee! / Junum din mubaa-ruq ho! / Saal-gi-rah mubaa-ruq ho!)

▶ A very happy wedding anniversary!
Shādi kī varshgānTh ki bahut-bahut badhāi!
शादी की वर्षगाँठ की बहुत-बहुत बधाई!
(Shaa-dee kee ver-sh-gaan-Thh kee bahu-t-bahu-t budh-aa-ee!)

TOP DESTINATIONS IN INDIA

With its more than five thousand years of history, India has long attracted explorers from all over the world seeking the spices of life and the colors of the rainbow.

▶ Agra Fort, Taj Mahal, Fateh Pur Sikri Agra
Āgré kā qilā, Tāj Mahal, Fateh Pur Sikri, Āgrā
आगरे का क़िला, ताज महल, फ़तहपुर सीकरी, आगरा
(Aag-ray kaa qi-laa, Taaj Ma-hel, Futeh pore seek-ree, Aag-raa)

▶ Ajanta, Ellora and Elephanta caves, Maharshtra
Ajantā, Ellorā aur Elephantā kī guphāyé, Mahārāshtra
अजन्ता, एलोरा और एलीफ़ैन्टा की गुफ़ाएँ, महाराष्ट्र
(Uj-untaa, Al-oraa aur Alee-phantaa kee gufaa-yen, Ma-haa-raash-traa)

▶ Beaches, churches and convents of Goa
Goā ké taT, girijāghar aur convents
गोआ के तट गिरिजाघर और कॉन्वैन्ट्स
(Goa kay tuT, Gi-re-jaa-ghar aur convents)

► Buddhist Monuments at Sanchi, Uttar Pradesh
Sānchī ké baudh stūp साँची के बौद्ध स्तूप
(Saanchee kay baw-dh st-oop)

► Backwater rides / whitewater rafting, Kerela (The backwaters are a network of canals, bayous, rivers, and other waterways that total more than 900 km in length.)

► Great Living Chola Temples, Tamil Nadu
Mahān Chol Mandir, Tamil Nādu महान चोल मंदिर
(Mah-haan Cho-l Mun-dir)

► Group of Monuments Khajuraho, Hampi and Mahabalipuram in Madhya Pradesh and Maharshtra
Madhya Pradesh aur Maharashtra mein Kjajurā ho, Hampi aur Mahābalipuram ke smarak मध्य प्रदेश और महाराष्ट्र में खजुराहो, हम्पी और महाबलीपुरम के स्मारक
(Madh-ya pr-deish aur Mahaa-raash-tr mein Khaju-raaho, Hump-ee aur Mahaa-bulli-pur-um kay smaa-ruck)

► Red Fort, Humayun's Tomb, Qutub Minar, Delhi
Dillī kā lāl quilā, Humāyů̃ kā muqbarā, Qutub minār दिल्ली का लाल क़िला, हुमायूँ का मक़्बरा, क़ुतुब मीनार *(Dill-ee kaa laal qui-laa, Human-yoon kaa muq-burraa, Qu-tub mee-naar)*

► Kazironga, Keolodeo, Sundarbans National Park
Kāzirangā, Kéolādeo, Sundarban rāshtriya Udyān काज़ीरंगा, केवलादेव और सुंदरबन राष्ट्रीय उद्यान
(Kaa-zee-rung-aa, Kev-laa-dave, Sunder-bun rash-triy udyaan)

▶ Wildlife sanctuaries
Vanyajīv AbhyāraNya वन्यजीव अभ्यारण्य
(One-ny-jeev abh-yaa-ruN-y)

▶ Forts, palaces and sand dunes of Rajasthan
Rajasthān ké garDh, mahal aur rét ké tīlé
राजस्थान के गढ़, महल और रेत के टीले
(Raaj-us-thaan kay gur-Dh, muh-hul aur ray-t kay tea-lay)

▶ Rock Shelters of Bhimbetka (Stone Age)
Bhīmbétkā ké pāshārN Āshraya
भीम-बेटका के पाषाण आश्रय
(Bheem-Bait-kaa kay paashaarN aash-ruy)

▶ Temples of India (East, West, North and South)
Bhārat ké mandir भारत के मंदिर
(Bhaa-rat kay mun-dir)

▶ Natural Beauty of North and East India (Kashmir, Uttranchal, Tibbet, Assam, Manipur)
Uttar aur Pūrv Bhārat kī prākritik sundartā
उत्तर और पूर्वी भारत की प्राकृतिक सुंदरता
(Utt-er aur Poorv Bhaa-rat kay praa-kri-tik sun-der-taa)

▶ Andamna and Nicobar Islands (in the Bay of Bengal)
Bengāl kī khārDī mein Andmān aur Nicobār Dweep Samūh
बंगाल की खाड़ी में अंडमान और निकोबार द्वीप समूह
(Bung-aal kee khaa-rDee mein Und-maan aur Nick-o-baar Dweep Sum-ooh)

SIGHTSEEING

holidays	**ChuTTiyā̃** छुट्टियाँ
	(ChuTT-iyaan)
vacation	**Avkāsh** अवकाश
	(avkaash)
tourist	**parytak** पर्यटक
	(per-ya-tuck)
place	**sthal / sthan / jagah**
	स्थल / स्थान / जगह
	(sth-ul / sth-aan / jug-uh)
tourist places	**parytak sthal** पर्यटक स्थल
	(per-ya-tuck sth-ul)
tourism	**paryatan** पर्यटन
	(pery-ton)
tourism department	**paryatan vibhāg** पर्यटन विभाग
	(per-y-ton vi-bhaag)
travel	**yātrā / safar** यात्रा / सफ़र
	(yaat-raa / suf-er)
traveler	**yātrī / musāfir** यात्री / मुसाफ़िर
	(yaat-ree / musaa-fir)
open	**khulā** खुला
	(khu-laa)
close	**band** बंद
	(bund)
office	**kāryālay / daftar** कार्यालय / दफ़्तर
	(kaar-yaa-luy / duft-er)
monument	**smārak** स्मारक
	(smaa-ruck)
remains	**avshésh** अवशेष
	(uv-shay-sh)

temple	**mandir** मंदिर *(mun-dir)*
mosque	**masjid** मस्जिद *(mus-jid)*
shrine of a Muslim Sufi saint	**dargāh** दरगाह *(der-gaah)*
fort	**garDh** गढ़ *(gerDh)*
palace	**mahal** महल *(mah-hel)*
ruins	**khandhar** खंडहर *(khund-her)*
tombs	**maqbarā** मक़बरा *(muq-burr-aa)*
garden	**bāgīchā** बाग़ीचा *(baagh-eechaa)*
park	**udyān** उद्यान *(ud-yaan)*
valley	**ghāṭī** घाटी *(ghaa-tee)*
museum	**sangrahālay** संग्रहालय *(sung-ruh-aalay)*
zoo	**chirDiyā ghar** चिड़िया घर *(chi-rDee-yaa ghar)*
parliament house	**sansad bhawan** संसद भवन *(sun-sudd bhuv-un)*
president's house	**rāshtrapati bhawan** राष्ट्रपति भवन *(raash-trua putti bhaw-un)*
embankments	**ghāṭ** घाट *(ghaaT)*

excursion	**charDhāyī** चढ़ाई *(cherDh-aayee)*
mountaineering	**parvatarohrN** पर्वतारोहण *(per-vut-aa-roharN)*
boat	**nāv** नाव *(naav)*
boat ride	**naukāyan** नौकायन *(knaw-kaa-yun)*
umbrella	**Chhātā** छाता *(Chhaa-taa)*
observatory	**védhshālā** वेधशाला *(way-dh-shaa-laa)*
planetarium	**nakshatra bhawan** नक्षत्र भवन *(nuksh-utr bhaw-un)*
historical	**étihāsik** ऐतिहासिक *(a-ti-haa-sik)*
cultural	**sānskritik** सांस्कृतिक *(saans-kri-tik)*
religious	**dhārmik** धार्मिक *(dhaar-mik)*
family	**pariwār** परिवार *(per-i-waar)*
children	**bachché** बच्चे *(buch-chay)*
group	**samūh** समूह *(sum-ooh)*
price	**mūlya / qīmat / dām** मूल्य / क़ीमत / दाम *(mool-y / qee-mut / daam)*
discount	**ChūT** छूट *(Chh-ooT)*

local	**sthānīya** स्थानीय *(sthaa-neeya)*
outsiders / foreigners	**bāhar sé āné wālé / vidéshī** बाहर से आने वाले / विदेशी *(baa-her say aa-nay waa-lay / vi-dei-she)*

▶ What time does the museum open?
Museum / Sangrahālay kitné bajé khultā hai?
म्यूज़ियम / संग्रहालय कितने बजे खुलता है?
(Museum / Sung-ra-haa-luy kit-nay buj-ay khul-taa hai?)

▶ What time does the tourist office close?
Paryatan vibhāg kā daftar kitné bajé band hotā hai? पर्यटन विभाग का दफ़्तर कितने बजे बंद होता है?
(Per-y-ton vi-bhaag kaa duft-er kit-nay buj-ay bund hotaa hai?)

▶ Are there any special tickets for foreign tourists?
Vidéshī yātriyő ké liyé koī vishésh ticket hai?
विदेशी यात्रियों के लिए कोई विशेष टिकट है?
(Vid-day-shee yaat-riyon kay liyay koi wish-ay-sh tick-ut hai?)

▶ May I take your photo?
Kyā mai(n) āpkī tasvīr lé lű?
क्या मैं आपकी तस्वीर ले लूँ?
(Kyaa main aap-key tus-veer lay loon?)

▶ Can you take our picture?
Kyā āp hamārī tasvīr khĭch dégé?
क्या आप हमारी तस्वीर खींच देंगे?
(Kyaa aap hum-aa-ree tus-veer kheench-dayn-gay?)

▶ Who had it built?
Yeh kisné banwāyā thā? यह किसने बनवाया था?
(Yeh kis-nay bun-waa-yaa thaa?)

▶ How old is it?
Yeh kitnā purānā hai? यह कितना पुराना है?
(Yeh kit-naa puraa-naa hai?)

▶ Where can I have my pictures developed?
Main yahă tasvirĕ kahă dhluwā saktā hŭ?
मैं यहाँ तस्वीरें कहाँ धुलवा सकता हूँ?
(Main ya-haan tus-vee-ren ka-haan dhul-waa suk-taa hoon?)

▶ What are the times of the tours?
Tour jāné kā kyā kyā samay hai?
टूर जाने का क्या-क्या समय है?
(Tour jaa-nay kaa kyaa-kyaa sum-ay hai?)

▶ Is there any tour guide available?
Kyā koī tour guide mілégā?
क्या कोई टूर गाइड मिलेगा?
(Kyaa koi tour guide mil-ay-gaa?)

PART SEVEN

Key Names & Signs

INDIA'S STATES & UNION TERRITORIES

THE 28 STATES

Andhra Pradesh आन्ध्र प्रदेश
  (Aan-dhra-pr-dai-sh)
Arunachal Pradesh अरुणाचल प्रदेश
  (Arun-aanch-ul Pr-dai-sh)
Assam आसाम
  (Aa-saam)
Bihar बिहार
  (Bi-haar)
Chattisgarh छत्तीसगढ़
  (Chhutt-is-garh)
Goa गोआ
  (Go-aa)
Gujarat गुजरात
  (Guj-raat)
Harayana हरियाणा
  (Hari-yaa-rNaa)
Himachal Pradesh हिमाचल प्रदेश
  (Him-aanch-ul Pr-dai-sh)
Jammu & Kashmir जम्मू और कश्मीर
  (Jum-moo & Kash-meer)

Jharkhand झारखंड
(Jhaar-khunD)
Karnatak कर्नाटक
(Ker-naa-tuk)
Kerel केरल
(Ker-e-laa)
Madhya Pradesh मध्य प्रदेश
(Mudh-ya Pr-dai-sh)
Maharashtra महाराष्ट्र
(Mahaa-raash-tr)
Manipur मणिपुर
(Mani-pur)
Mizoram मिज़ोरम
(Mi-zo-rum)
Nagaland नागालैंड
(Naa-gaa-land)
Orrisa उड़ीसा
(U-rDee-saa)
Punjab पंजाब
(Pun-jaab)
Rajasthan राजस्थान
(Raaj-us-thaan)
Sikkim सिक्किम
(Sik-kim)
Tamil Nadu तमिलनाडू
(Taa-mill naa-doo)
Tripura त्रिपुरा
(Tri-puraa)
Uttarakhand उत्तराखंड
(Utt-uraa-khund)
West Bengal पश्चिम बंगाल
(Pash-chim Bung-aal)

THE 7 UNION TERRITORIES

Andaman & Nicobar Islands
अंडमान और निकोबार द्वीप समूह
  (Und-maan & Nick-obaar i-land)
Chandigarh चंडीगढ़
  (Chun-dee-garDh)
The Government of NCT of Delhi
Dadar & Nagar Haveli दादर और नगर हवेली
  (Daa-der & Nug-er Huv-ay-lee)
Daman & Diu दमन और दीयू
  (Dum-un & Dee-yoo)
Lakshdweep लक्षद्वीप
  (Luck-sh-dweep)
Puducherry पुदूचेरी
  (Poo-doo-che-ry)

COMMON SIGNS

Knowing and understanding road signs and any other signs
in and on buildings is a very important language asset for
a foreign visitor to have. Here are few of the signs that you
may find in India.

Entrance	**pravésh dwār** प्रवेश द्वार
	(pra-way-sh dw-aar)
Exit	**nikās** निकास
	(nick-aas)
Push	**dhakkā dījiyé** धक्का दीजिए
	(dhuk-kaa dee-ji-yay)

Pull	**khīnchiyé** खींचिए *(kheench-i-yay)*
Emergency Exit	**āpāt dwār** आपात द्वार *(aap-aat dw-aar)*
Toilet	**shauchālay** शौचालय *(shaw-chaa-lay)*
Men	**purush** पुरुष *(pu-ru-sh)*
Women	**mahilā** महिला *(ma-hilaa)*
Open	**kulā hai** खुला है। *(khu-laa hai)*
Closed	**band hai** बंद है। *(bun-d hai)*
Danger	**khatrā** ख़तरा *(khut-raa)*
Beware	**sāvdhān** सावधान *(saav-dhaan)*
No smoking	**dhumra pān manā hai.** धूम्रपान मना है। *(dhoom-ra-paan mun-aa hai)*
Do not touch.	**Chhūnā manā hai.** छूना मना है। *(Chhoo-naa mun-aa hai)*
Information	**jānkārī** जानकारी *(jaan-kaa-ree)*
Complaints	**shikāyat** शिकायत *(shi-kaa-yat)*
Notice	**sūchnā** सूचना *(soo-ch-naa)*
Cashier	**khajānchī** खजांची *(khaj-aan-chee)*

▶ Please honk / Horn please
Kripayā horn dé कृपया हार्न दें|
(kri-pa-yaa horn dein)

▶ Parking Lot
GarDī kharDī karné kī jagah
गाड़ी खड़ी करने की जगह
(Gaa-rDee kha-rDee ker-nay kee jug-ah)

▶ Parking is prohibited here
Yahā̃ gārDī kharDī karnā manā hai.
यहाँ गाड़ी खड़ी करना मना है|
(Ya-haan gaa-rDee kha-eDee ker-naa mun-aa hai)

▶ Do not enter
Andar ānā manā hai. अन्दर आना मना है|
(Un-der aa-naa mun-aa hai)

Pravésh varjit hai. प्रवेश वर्जित है|
(Pr-way-sh ver-jit hai)

▶ No shoes in the temple
Mandir mei(n) jūté lé jānā manā hai
मंदिर में जूते ले जाना मना है|
(Mun-dir mein joo-tay lay jaa-naa mun-aa hai)

▶ Please take off your shoes outside
Kripyā jūté bāhar utāriyé कृपया जूते बाहर उतारिये
(Krip-yaa joo-tay baa-her utaa-re-yay)

ROAD SIGNS

speed **gati** गति
(ga-tee)

speed limit **gati sīmā** गति सीमा
(ga-tee see-maa)

red light **lāl battī** लाल बत्ती
(laal-but-tee)

green light **harī battī** हरी बत्ती
(hurry-but-tee)

yellow light **pīlī battī** पीली बत्ती
(peel-ee but-tee)

stop **rukiyé** रुकिए
(rook-e-yay)

caution, beware **sāvdhān** सावधान
(saav-dhaan)

intersection **chaurāhā** चौराहा
(chaw-raa-haa)

road **sarDak** सड़क
(sa-rD-k)

highway **rājmārg** राजमार्ग
(raaj-maa-rg)

grade **charDhāyī** चढ़ाई
(cha-rDh-aa-ee)

turn **morD** मोड़
(mow-rD)

roundabout **ghumāv** घुमाव
(ghu-maav)

Entrance Prohibited **pravésh varjit hai**
प्रवेश वर्जित है
(pra-vei-sh ver-jit hai)

PART EIGHT

Additional Vocabulary

FOOD TERMS

almond	**bādām** बादाम *(baa-daam)*
apple	**séb** सेब *(say-b)*
banana	**kélā** केला *(kay-laa)*
beans	**phalī** फली *(phulee)*
beet root	**chukandar** चुकन्दर *(chook-under)*
black pepper	**kālī mirch (kaal-ee mirch)** काली मिर्च
butter	**makkhan** मक्खन *(muck-khun)*
cabbage	**band gobhī** बन्द गोभी *(bund-go-bhee)*
cardamom	**ilāychī** इलायची *(ilaay-chee)*
carrot	**gājar** गाजर *(gaa-jer)*
cashew	**kājū** काजू *(kaa-joo)*

cauliflower	**phūl gobhī** फूल गोभी
	(phool-go-bhee)
chick pea	**chanā** चना
	(chun-aa)
chicken	**murgī** मुर्गी
	(mur-gee)
chili powder	**pisī mirch** पिसी मिर्च
	(pisee mirch)
cinnamon	**dāl-chīnī** दाल चीनी
	(daal-chee-nee)
cloves	**long** लौंग
	(law-ng)
coriander	**dhaniā** धनिया
	(dhun-iyaa)
corn	**makkā** मक्का
	(muck-kaa)
cream of wheat	**sujī** सूजी
	(soo-jee)
cucumber	**khīrā** खीरा
	(khee-raa)
cumin	**girā** जीरा
	(jee-raa)
curd / yogurt	**dahī** दही
	(da-hee)
eggplant	**bangan** बैंगन
	(bang-un)
fenugreek	**méthī** मेथी
	(may-thee)
fish	**maChlī** मछली
	(muCh-lee)

flour (whole wheat)	**ātā** आटा *(aa-taa)*
flour, all purpose (white)	**maidā** मैदा *(mey-daa)*
fruit	**phal** फल *(ph-ul)*
garlic	**lehsun** लहसुन *(leh-su-n)*
ginger	**adrak** अदरक *(ud-ruck)*
grapes	**angūr** अंगूर *(ung-oor)*
green pea	**matar** मटर *(mutter)*
guava	**amrūd** अमरूद *(um-rood)*
honey	**shahad** शहद *(shu-hudd)*
kidney beans	**rājmā** राजमा *(raaj-maa)*
lemon	**nībū** नीबू *(nee-boo)*
lentil	**dāl** दाल *(daal)*
mango	**ām** आम *(aam)*
mango powder	**amchūr** अमचूर *(um-choor)*
mint	**pudinā** पुदीना *(pu-dee-naa)*

mustard	**sarsõ** सरसों *(sir-sawn)*
oil	**tale** तेल *(tay-l)*
onion	**pyāz** प्याज़ *(pyaa-z)*
orange	**santrā** संतरा *(sunt-raa)*
papaya	**papītā** पपीता *(puppy-taa)*
peanut	**mūngphalī** मूँगफली *(moong-phulee)*
pear	**nāshpātī** नाशपाती *(naash-paa-tee)*
pineapple	**annānās** अन्नानास *(un-naa-naas)*
plum	**ārDū** आड़ू *(aa-rDoo)*
pomegranate	**anār** अनार *(un-aar)*
potato	**ālū** आलू *(aa-loo)*
pumpkin	**kaddū** कद्दू *(kud-doo)*
radish	**mūlī** मूली *(moo-lee)*
raisin	**kishmish** किशमिश *(kish-mish)*
rice	**chāval** चावल *(chaa-vul)*

salt	**namak** नमक
	(num-uck)
sesame	**til** तिल
	(till)
spice	**masālā** मसाला
	(mus-aa-laa)
spinach	**pālak** पालक
	(paa-luck)
sugar	**chīnī / shakkar** चीनी
	(chee-knee / shuck-ker)
sweet potato	**shakarkand** शकरकन्द
	(shuck-ker-kund)
tamarind	**imlī** इमली
	(im-lee)
tea	**chai** चाय
	(chaa-y)
tomato	**tamātar** टमाटर
	(tum-aa-ter)
turmeric	**haldī** हल्दी
	(hull-dee)
turnip	**shalgam** शलगम
	(shul-gum)
vegetable	**sabzī** सब्ज़ी
	(sub-zee)
walnut	**akhrote** अखरोट
	(ukh-rote)
watermelon	**tarbūz** तरबूज़
	(ter-booze)
yogurt	**dahī** दही
	(da-hee)

GENERAL WORD LIST

A

accident	**durghtnā** दुर्घटना *(dur-ghut-naa)*
accommodation	**rehné kī jagah** रहने की जगह *(reh-nay kee jug-ah)*
address	**patā** पता *(putt-taa)*
air conditioning	**vātānukūlit** वातानुकुलित *(vaa-taa nu-cool-it)*
airport	**hawāi aDDā** हवाई अड्डा *(hawaai uD-Daa)*
airmail	**hawāi dāk** हवाई डाक *(hawaai Daak)*
alcohol	**sharāb** शराब *(sha-raab)*
American	**amrīkī** अमरीकी *(um-re-kee)*
appointment	**samay lénā** समय लेना *(sum-ay lay-naa)*
art	**kalā** कला *(ka-laa)*
assault	**hamlā** हमला *(hum-laa)*

B

baby	**bachchā** बच्चा *(buch-chaa)*
baby sitter	**āyā** आया *(aa-yaa)*

bachelor/ unmarried	**kŭwārā** (for a male) / **-rī** (for a female) कुँवारा *(kun-waa-raa / -ree)*
baggage	**sāmān** सामान *(saa-maan)*
bathroom	**gusalkhānā** गुसलखाना *(gusal-khaa-naa)*
bicycle	**cykil** साइकिल *(cy-kil)*
big	**barDā** बड़ा *(burDaa)*
bill	**bill** बिल *(bill)*
black	**kālā** काला *(kaa-laa)*
blue	**nīlā** नीला *(nee-laa)*
boy	**larDkā** लड़का *(lerD-kaa)*
branch (office)	**shākhā** शाखा *(shaa-khaa)*
bread	**double rotī** डबल रोटी *(double-row-tee)*
breakfast	**nāshtā** नाश्ता *(naash-taa)*
briefcase	**attaichī** अटैची *(ut-tai-chee)*
broken	**tūtā huā** टूटा हुआ *(tootaa-huaa)*
brown	**bhūrā** भूरा *(bhoo-raa)*
burglar	**chore** चोर *(chore)*

bus stop	**bus aDDā** बस अड्डा *(bus-uD-Daa)*
business	**vyāpār** व्यापार *(vyaa-paar)*

C

café	**jalpāngrigh** जलपानगृह *(jull-paan-grih)*
camel	**ūnT** ऊँट *(oonT)*
camera (digital)	**camera**
cancelled	**radd** रद्द *(rudd)*
canopy	**Chhatrī** छतरी *(Chhut-ree)*
capital (money)	**pūnjī** पूँजी *(poon-jee)*
car	**gārDī** गाड़ी *(gaa-rDee)*
card (playing)	**tāsh** ताश *(taash)*
cash	**nakad** नक़द *(nuqud)*
change (coins)	**khullé** खुल्ले *(khull-lay)*
cheap	**sastā** सस्ता *(sus-taa)*
child	**bachchā** बच्चा *(buch-chaa)*
children	**bachché** बच्चे *(buch-chay)*

Christian	**isāyī** इसाई
	(isaa-yee)
church	**girijāghar** गिरिजाघर
	(giri-jaa ghar)
clean	**sāf** साफ़
	(saaf)
clock	**gharDī** घड़ी
	(gherD-ee)
clothes	**kaprDé** कपड़े
	(kup-rDay)
comb	**kgghā** कंघा
	(kung-ghaa)
confirm (a ticket, room)	**pakkā** पक्का
	(puck-kaa)

D

date of birth	**janm tithī** जन्म तिथि
	(junm ti-thee)
daughter	**bétī** बेटी
	(bay-tee)
delay	**dérī** देरी
	(day-ree)
departure	**prasthān** प्रस्थान
	(pr-us-taan)
deposit	**jamā karnā** जमा करना
	(jumaa ker-naa)
dirty	**gandā** गन्दा
	(gun-daa)
document	**kāgzāt / dastāwéz** कागज़ात / दस्तावेज़
	(kaag-zaat / dust-aa-ways)
door	**darwāzā** दरवाज़ा
	(der-waa-zaa)

driver	**chālak** चालक
	(chaa-luck)
drugs	**nashīlé / mādak padārth**
	नशीले / मादक पदार्थ
	(nush-ee-lay / maa-duk pud-aarth)
drunk	**nashé mei(n)** नशे में
	(nush-a mein)

E

earthquake	**bhū kamp** भूकंप
	(bhoo-kump)
eat out	**bāhar khānā** बाहर खाना
	(baa-her khaa-naa)
electricity	**bijlī** बिजली
	(bij-lee)
elephant	**hāthī** हाथी
	(haa-thee)
elevator	**lift** लिफ़्ट
	(lifT)
e-mail	**e-mail**
embassy	**dutāvās** दूतावास
	(doot-aavaas)
emergency	**āpātkāl** आपातकाल
	(aapaat-kaal)
entrance	**pravésh** प्रवेश
	(pr-way-sh)
exchange	**badalnā, ādān-pradān**
	बदलना, आदान प्रदान
	(bud-ul-naa, aa-daan-pra-daan)
exercise	**vyāyām** व्यायाम
	(vyaa-yaam)
exit	**nikās** निकास
	(ni-kaas)

F

family	**pariwār** परिवार
	(peri-waar)
fan	**p̣akhā** पंखा
	(punk-khaa)
fax	**fax**
fee	**shulk** शुल्क
	(shulk)
festival	**tyohār** त्योहार
	(tyo-haar)
fire	**āg** आग
	(aag)
first	**péhlá / péhlī / péhlé**
	पहला / पहली / पहले
	(peh-laa / peh-lee / peh-lay)
fixed price	**niyat mulya / tay dām**
	नियत मूल्य / तय दाम
	(ni-yut moo-ly / tuy daam)
fight	**larDāī** लड़ाई
	(lerD-aa-ee)
flight	**urDān** उड़ान
	(urDaan)
floor, story	**manzil** मंज़िल
(of a building)	*(mun-zil)*
folk art	**lok kalā** लोक कला
	(lok kalaa)
foreigner	**videśhī** विदेशी
	(vid-a-shee)
forgive me	**māf kījiyé** माफ़ कीजिए
	(maaf-key-g-yay)
friend (male)	**mitra / dost** मित्र / दोस्त
	(mi-tr / tho-st)

friend (female)	**sahélī** सहेली
	(sa-hay-lee)
fun	**mazā** मज़ा
	(muz-aa)

G

gas station	**pétrol pump** पैट्रोल पंप
	(pet-role pump)
gift	**uphār** उपहार
	(up-haar)
girl	**larDkī** लड़की
	(lerD-kee)
guide	**mārgdarshak** मार्गदर्शक
	(maarg-der-shuck)

H

handicrafts	**hastkalā** हस्तकला
	(hust-kul-aa)
handmade	**hāth kā banā huā** हाथ का बना हुआ
	(haath-kaa bun-aa hu-aa)
headache	**sir dard** सिर दर्द
	(s-ir der-d)
heavy	**bhārī** भारी
	(bhaa-ree)
highway	**rājmārg** राजमार्ग
	(raaj-maarg)
hobby	**ruchi / shauq** रुचि / शौक़
	(ru-chi / shocq)
holiday (time off, vacation)	**ChhuTTī / avkāsh** छुट्टी / अवकाश
	(ChhuT-Tea / uv-kaash)
holiday (celebration)	**tyohār / parv** त्योहार / पर्व
	(tyo-haar / perv)

home	**ghar / grih** घर / गृह *(gh-ar / gri-huh)*
hot	**garm / garam** गर्म / गरम *(ger-m / ga-rum)*
hungry (adj)	**bhūkhā / bhūkhī / bhūkhé** भूखा /भूखी / भूखे *(bhoo-khaa / bhoo-khee / bhoo-khay)*
hurry up	**jaldī karo / jaldī kījiye** जल्दी करो / कीजिए *(j-ull-dee ker-o / j-ull-dee ki-g-yay)*
husband	**pati** पति *(putt-i)*

I

ice	**barf** बर्फ़ *(berr-f)*
identification	**péhchān / shinākht** पहचान / शिनाख़्त *(peh-chaan / shin-aakht)*
ill	**bīmār / aswasth** बीमार / अस्वस्थ *(bee-maar / uswus-th)*
illegal	**avaidh** अवैध *(uv-ai-dh)*
India	**Bhārat / Hindustan** भारत / हिन्दुस्तान *(Bhaa-rat / Hin-dus-taan)*
Indians (as a people)	**Bhartīya** भारतीय *(bhaar-teeya)*
iron	**lohā** लोहा *(lo-haa)*

J

jaggery (unrefined sugar)	**gurD** गुड़ *(gu-rD)*

jail	**kārāgār** कारागार *(kaa-raa-gaar)*
Jew	**yahūdī** यहूदी *(y-hoo-dee)*
jewelry	**géhné** गहने *(gah-nay)*
joke	**chuTkulā / latīfā** चुटकुला / लतीफ़ा *(chuT-kulaa / lut-ee-faa)*
journal	**dainikī / roznāmchā** *(dah-ni-kee / rose-naam-chaa)* दैनिकी / रोज़नामचा
journey	**yātrā / safar** यात्रा / सफ़र *(yaat-raa / suffer)*

K

key	**chābī** चाबी *(chaa-bee)*
knife	**chākū** चाकू *(chaa-koo)*
kidnapping	**aphararN** अपहरण *(up-her-raN)*
kind (person)	**dayālū** दयालु *(duy-aa-lu)*
kiss	**chumban** चुम्बन *(chum-bun)*
kitchen	**rasoī** रसोई *(russ-oee)*
knitting	**bunāi** बुनाई *(bu-naa-ee)*

L

lad (boy)	**larDkā** लड़का *(lerD-kaa)*

lamp (earthen, clay)	**dīpak** दीपक *(dee-puck)*
language	**bhāshā** भाषा *(bhaa-shaa)*
laptop (computer)	**laptop**
large	**vishāl / barDā** विशाल / बड़ा *(wish-aal / ber-Daa)*
last	**akhirī** आख़िरी *(aa-khi-ree)*
late	**dérī sé** देरी से *(dayr-ee say)*
later	**bād mei(n)** बाद में *(baad mein)*
laundry	**dhulāī** धुलाई *(dhu-laa-ee)*
leopard	**chītā** चीता *(chee-taa)*
lion	**shér** शेर *(shay-r)*
lock	**tālā** ताला *(taa-laa)*
loan	**udhār / rirN** उधार / ऋण *(oo-dhaar / rirN)*
love	**pyār** प्यार *(pyaar)*

M

| ma'am | **mahodayā** महोदया
 (maho-da-uh-yaa) |
| magazine | **patrikā** पत्रिका
 (putt-rick-aa) |

mail	**dāk** डाक
	(daak)
man	**ādmī / purush** आदमी / पुरुष
	(aad-mee / pur-oosh)
management	**prabhandhan** प्रबन्धन
	(prub-un-dhun)
mandatory	**zarūrī / anivāry** ज़रूरी / अनिवार्य
	(zer-oo-re / un-i-vaa-rya)
market	**bāzār** बाज़ार
	(baa-zaar)
married	**shādi shudā** शादी शुदा
	(shaa-dee shu-daa)
mausoleum	**maqbarā** मक़बरा
	(muq-berra)
memory	**yād / smriti** याद / स्मृति
	(yaad / sm-riti)
memory card (camera)	**memory card**
meeting	**baiThak / sabhā** बैठक / सभा
	(ba-Thh-uck/sub-haa)
milk	**dūdh** दूध
	(doo-dh)
mosquito	**machChhar** मच्छर
	(much-Chher)
mouse	**chūhā** चूहा
	(choo-haa)
murder	**hatyā** हत्या
	(hut-yaa)
music	**sangeet** संगीत
	(sung-eet)

mistake	**galtī** ग़लती *(gull-tee)*
monkey	**bander** बन्दर *(bun-der)*
monk	**sādhū** साधु *(saa-dhoo)*
morning	**subah** सुबह *(sub-eh)*
mosque	**masjid** मसजिद *(mus-jid)*

N

nanny	**āyā** आया *(aa-yaa)*
name	**nām** नाम *(naam)*
nausea	**matlī** मतली *(mut-lee)*
near	**pās** पास *(paas)*
necessary	**zarurī, avashyak** ज़रूरी, आवश्यक *(zer-oo-re / aav-ush-yuck)*
needle	**suī** सुई *(sue-ee)*
neither	**dono hi nahī** दोनों ही नहीं *(tho-knaw hee naheen)*
new	**nayā / nayī / nayé** नया / नयी / नये *(na-yaa / na-yee / na-yay)*
news	**khabar / samāchār** ख़बर / समाचार *(khubb-er / sum-aa-chaar)*

newspaper	**akhbār / samāchār patra** अख़बार / समाचार पत्र *(uckh-baar / sum-aa-chaar put-r)*
night	**rāt / rātrī** रात / रात्रि *(raat / raat-ri)*
noise	**shor** शोर *(shore)*

O

obstetrician	**prasutirog vishéshagya** प्रसूति रोग विशेषज्ञ *(pr-soo-tee row-g wish-a-sh-ugy)*
office	**daftar/ kāryālay** दफ़्तर, कार्यालय *(duf-ter / kaar-yaa-ly)*
open (adj)	**khulā / khulī / khulé** खुला / खुली / खुले *(khu-laa / khu-lee / khul-ay)*
orange	**nārangi, santrā** नारंगी, संतरा *(naa-rung-ee, sun-t-raa)*

P

paper	**kāgaz** काग़ज़ *(kaa-guz)*
parents	**mātā-pitā, abhibhāvak** माता-पिता, अभिभावक *(maa-taa-pitaa, ubhi-bhaa-vuck)*
partner	**sājhédār** साझेदार *(saa-jh-a daar)*
pen	**qalam, lékhnī** क़लम, लेखनी *(qul-um, lay-kh-nee)*
pillow	**takiyā** तक़िया *(tucq-iyaa)*

pill	**golī** गोली
	(go-lee)
post office	**dāk ghar** डाकघर
	(daak-ghar)
present (gift)	**uphār, bhéT** उपहार, भेंट
	(up-haar, bhen-T)
problem	**samasyā, paréshānī** समस्या,
	परेशानी
	(sum-us-yaa, per-a-shaa-nee)
price	**dām, qimat, mūly, bhāv**
	दाम, कीमत, मूल्य, भाव
	(daam, qee-mut, mool-ya, bhaav)

Q

question	**sawāl, prashan** सवाल, प्रश्न
	(suw-aal, pra-shn)
quickly	**jaldī sé, shīghratā sé** जल्दी से, शीघ्रता से
	(jal-dee say, she-ghra-taa say)
quilt	**razāī** रज़ाई
	(ruz-aa-ee)

R

rain	**bārish** बारिश
	(baa-rish)
reason	**kāraN** कारण
	(kaa-ruN)
religious	**dhārmik** धार्मिक
	(dhaar-mick)
relative	**rishtédār, sambandhī**
	रिश्तेदार, संबंधी
	(rish-tay-daar, sum-bun-dhee)
rent	**kirāyā** किराया
	(qi-raa-yaa)

road	**sarDak, mārg** सड़क, मार्ग *(serD-uck, maar-g)*
room	**kamrā, kāksh** कमरा, कक्ष *(kum-raa, kuk, sh)*
river	**nadī** नदी *(na-dee)*
right (direction)	**băyā, băyī** बाँया, बाँई *(baan-yaa, baan-yee)*
right (correct)	**sahī, Thhīk** सही, ठीक *(sa-hee, Thh-eek)*

S

school	**vidyālay** विद्यालय *(vidyaa-lay)*
shirt	**qamīz** कमीज़ *(qum-eez)*
shoe	**jūtā** जूता *(joo-taa)*
shop	**dukān** दुकान *(du-kaan)*
shop keeper	**dukāndār** दुकानदार *(du-kaan-daar)*
sign	**pratīk, chinnh** प्रतीक / चिन्ह *(pra-teek, chin-h)*
smile	**muskurāhaT** मुसकुराहट *(mus-ku-raa-huT)*
Skype (verb)	**skype**
sleep	**nīnd** नींद *(neen-d)*
smoking	**dhūmrpān** धूम्रपान *(dhoomr-paan)*

snake	**săp** साँप
	(saanp)
soap	**sābun** साबुन
	(saa-bu-n)
spoon	**chamach** चम्मच
	(chum-uch)
stain	**dāg, dhabbā** दाग़, धब्बा
	(daag, dhub-baa)
student	**vidyārthī, Chhātra** विद्यार्थी, छात्र
	(vidyaar-thee, Chhaat-ra)
sweet	**mīThhā** मीठा
	(mee-Thhaa)

T

tasty	**swādishT** स्वादिष्ट
	(swaad-ishT)
tea	**chāi** चाय
	(chaa-y)
talk	**bātchīt** बातचीत
	(baat-cheet)
table	**méz** मेज़
	(maze)
temple	**mandir** मंदिर
	(mun-dir)
text, texting (electronic)	**text, texting**
thirst	**pyās** प्यास
	(pyaas)
thirsty	**pyāsā** प्यासा
	(pyaa-saa)
thanks	**dhanyavād** धन्यवाद
	(dh-uny-vaad)
today	**āj** आज
	(aaj)

tomorrow	**kal** कल
	(ka-ul)
tradition	**paramparā** परंपरा
	(per-um-per-aa)
train	**rail gārDī** रेल गाड़ी
	(rail-gaa-rDee)
translation	**anuvād** अनुवाद
	(anu-waad)
trash	**kūrDā** कूड़ा
	(koo-rDaa)

U

umbrella	**Chhāta, Chhatrī** छाता, छतरी
	(Chhaa-taa, Chhut-ree)
university	**viswavidyālay** विश्वविद्यालय
	(wishwa-vidyaa-lay)
under	**nīché** नीचे
	(nee-chay)

V

vacation	**ChhuTTī** छुट्टी
	(Chhu-TT-ee)
vegetarian	**shākahārī** शाकाहारी
	(shaa-kaa-haa-ree)
vehicle	**vāhan** वाहन
	(vaa-hun)
video, DVD	**video**

W

wallet	**baTuā** बटुआ
	(but-uaa)
wait	**intzār, pratiksha** इंतज़ार, प्रतीक्षा
	(int-zaar, pra-teek-shaa)

war	**yuddha** युद्ध
	(yuddh)
water	**pānī, jal** पानी, जल
	(paa-nee, jull)
web site	**web site**
week	**saptāh** सप्ताह
	(sup-taah)
welcome	**swāgat** स्वागत
	(swaa-gat)
west	**pūrv** पूर्व
	(poo-rv)
wet	**gīlā** गीला
	(gee-laa)
wife	**patni** पत्नि
	(putt-nee)
window	**khirDkī** खिड़की
	(khirD-kee)
woman	**aurat, mahilā** औरत, महिला
	(awe-rut, muh-hilaa)
worship	**pujā** पूजा
	(poo-jaa)

Y

year	**sāl, varsh** साल, वर्ष
	(saal, versh)
yesterday	**kal** कल
	(kull)
yes	**jī** जी
	(jee)

Z

zero	**shūnya** शून्य
	(shoo-ny)